history a IF SCH ce

# CHARTISTS CHARTISM *and*

## Joe Finn

The cover illustration is "Work" by Ford Maddox Brown, 1865 (courtesy Manchester City Art Galleries).

*British Library Cataloguing-in-Publication data*
Finn, Joe
  Chartists and chartism. – (History at source)
  I. Title   II. Series
  942.081

  ISBN 0–340–55623–4

First published 1992

| Impression number | 6 | 5 | 4 | 3 | 2 |
|---|---|---|---|---|---|
| Year | | 1999 | 1998 | 1997 | 1996 | 1995 |

Printed in Great Britain for Hodder & Stoughton Educational, a division of Hodder Headline Plc, 338 Euston Road, London NW1 3BH by Redwood Books, Trowbridge, Wiltshire.

# CONTENTS

# LIST OF MAPS AND TABLES

# APPROACHING SOURCE-BASED

# QUESTIONS

The aim of this book is to provide a set of key documents illustrating the Chartist movement and to suggest how the material can best be analysed and interpreted.

Questions based on documents and sources now form a compulsory part of all A level boards' papers. Many boards include such questions in their outline courses and all make source material questions a dominant feature of their depth studies, in which it is usual for as much as 50 per cent of the total marks to be allocated to the document section. The questions set vary; some boards require candidates to study prescribed texts, extracts from which appear on the exam paper for analysis. Other boards suggest a wider range of source material for study without indicating specific texts; detailed questions are then set on document extracts which will not necessarily have been seen previously, but which candidates should be able to analyse by reference to their knowledge of the course.

Some questions are essentially a comprehension exercise, testing the candidate's ability to read and understand a historical document. Others examine candidates' background knowledge of wider themes or probe their understanding of special topics. The most demanding are those which ask for evaluation of a historical document.

All examination papers indicate the number of marks on offer. These are a clear guide to the relative importance of the question in the exam paper and show what proportion of the candidates' time should be spent on it. As a rule of thumb, it is worth bearing in mind that for each mark offered there should be a corresponding point of fact or analysis; this is a broad, working guide and should not be followed slavishly. It is not suggested that candidates should waste valuable time and effort trying to find an artificial extra point of their own merely to satisfy an apparent numerical requirement.

Care should be taken to deal with the question as set. An examinee asked to evaluate the significance of a document will gain little simply from paraphrasing it or giving irrelevant details about its background. As well as showing understanding of sources, candidates are expected at this level to have an appreciation of historiography; that is, to know something about the problems in writing history. Being able to spot bias, attitude and motive in the writer of a given extract is important. Questions requiring comment on the 'tone' or the 'colour' of a passage are not uncommon. Certain general pointers are worth noting here. When asked to comment on 'tone' or 'colour', candidates should ask themselves such questions as: Is the writer of the extract evidently angry, bitter, confident, detached, involved? Is the document an official report or a personal reminiscence? Does the passage suggest that it is being written for a particular audience or is it a general statement? Is it propaganda or objective reporting? If candidates train themselves to pose such questions on the sources they study, they will develop the type of observational and analytical skills that merit high marks.

Another consideration, of no small account to A level examinees, is that a good grounding in document-based work, which broadens their knowledge and sharpens their appreciation of historical material, will prove of inestimable benefit in their handling of the essay part of the paper. The virtues of this 'knock-on' effect are very apparent to the examiners, as witness this comment from one of their reports: 'It is most unlikely that A or B grades would be awarded to candidates who could not show an awareness of the importance of first sources and an ability to quote relevantly from them'.

Candidates will handle source-based questions effectively if they have a sound technique. Such a technique requires understanding of both the documents and the questions. A serious error in the exam room is to look immediately at the questions and then scan the documents for the answers. Candidates who do this will find that they have answered a later question in responding to an earlier one, because they are unaware of the requirements of the questions as a whole. The reaction to this may be either to repeat the point in the later question, or look around for another. This too can be wrong and a sense of mounting panic besets the examinee.

The solution is to approach the exercise calmly and methodically. Time is allowed for reading, and candidates are well advised to use it fully. Reading the passages carefully has the advantage that it gives candidates a few minutes to steady nerves. More important, it enables them to understand the documents. Looking at the questions first must be avoided, for a knowledge of the questions will tempt candidates to skim the documents, seeking the answers at their first reading and impairing their understanding. If the material is difficult more than two readings may be necessary. Only when they fully understand the documents should examinees look at the questions, which should be read through once. A further reading of the extracts should then follow. The answers to the questions will then begin to emerge from the documents. A second reading of the questions should then be made. Only when candidates are confident that they understand what they are required to do, should they begin to respond on paper. A methodical approach such as this will enable examinees to take control of the exercise and impose their own pace upon it.

To summarise this approach:

1. DO NOT LOOK AT THE QUESTIONS.

2. Read the extracts for analysis *at least* twice.
3. Read through the questions once.
4. Read through the extracts again.
5. Read through the questions again.
6. Now, and not before, begin to respond in writing.

In the following introduction the numbers in square brackets refer to the chapter where the material under discussion is to be found.

# INTRODUCTION

In 1837 a working-class movement emerged in Britain which became known as Chartism. Two decades of activity followed, beginning with the drafting of a petition to parliament by the London Working Men's Association (LWMA). The petition made six demands for political change: universal manhood suffrage; annual parliaments; equal electoral districts; secret ballot; payment of MPs; the abolition of property qualifications for MPs. [1.C] These demands became known as the People's Charter, reminiscent of the Great Charter (Magna Carta) of 1215. Its supporters were styled Chartists and the high peaks of their activities were the three occasions when they submitted petitions to parliament seeking the implementation of the six points; that of June 1839, backed by 1.28 million signatures; that of May 1842, with 3.3 million; and that of April 1848, when six million signatures were claimed to support it, although under scrutiny there turned out to be just short of two million. [1.] The Chartist years closed in February 1858, when the last Chartist conference to be held voted to co-operate with moderate radical liberals. [1.] In doing so, this Chartist rump accepted that the movement had run its course. Over the following 70 years their demands were to be conceded, with the sole exception of annual parliaments. In truth the movement had died before 1858, although the claim by government and press that it died immediately after the failure of the 1848 petition was premature, for it survived and was vital for some years after that. [1.]

In not achieving their six demands during those years the Chartists came to be regarded as a failure, but this does not mean that they are without historical significance. [10.] Britain had been subjected sporadically to intense social disorder for many centuries; the Peasants' Revolt of 1381 had been such an outburst, when the lower orders of society had protested against oppression by their 'betters', and it was the primary aim of government policy during the sixteenth century to maintain social order. Certainly, fear of riot and tumult had been at the forefront of politicians' minds since the Tudor period. The Gordon Riots of the late eighteenth century, the Luddite disturbances of the early nineteenth and the Swing Riots of the 1830s had all served to stress in the minds of the propertied classes the awesome threat of unrest when the lower classes became alienated or disaffected from society. This fear had been underlined by the French Revolutions of 1789 and 1830.

Riot and tumult were not unfamiliar, therefore, when the Chartist General Convention met in London in February 1839 to prepare for the presentation of the petition and to decide upon what actions to take if parliament rejected it. [1.] What distinguishes Chartism from earlier incidents of unrest was that it became nationally organised and had clearly expressed objectives. [1.,2.] In addition, it was a mass movement comprising a large proportion of the working classes, supported more in the manufacturing communities than in the urban centres, and stronger in the provinces than in the capital. [5.]

The economic background to Chartism was one of change. Three processes, in train in the 1830s, were eventually to transform the face of Britain. Population was increasing at a rate which many observers regarded as alarming and not a few as catastrophic. This growth in population was becoming concentrated in expanding urban centres such as Birmingham, Leeds, Manchester and Glasgow. The mechanisation of production affected the traditional practices of work. By the late 1830s these processes had begun to have a serious impact upon the lives of the labouring classes; the concentration of population increased the risks to health through poor sewerage and contaminated water supplies. The factories and mills had begun to dominate the manufacturing communities, imposing new disciplines of long hours and low wages upon workers who included increasingly women and children. Perhaps more important, the traditional skills and crafts like nail-making and hand-loom weaving were subjected to fierce competition from machines, which drove down the earnings of the older crafts and forced these outworkers to work longer hours. Worse still, were the longer periods of unemployment which these workers were forced to endure. In times of slack trade the outworker was more easily dispensed with than the less skilled factory hand. [9.]

By the 1840s these changes still had some way to go before completion and it is easy to exaggerate their extent in the Chartist years. Nevertheless, they were sufficiently advanced by 1840 for the most affected workers to be acutely aware of the changes they were experiencing in their lives. Apart from the impact on the standard of living of the labouring class, a hotly debated question among historians [10.], there was a loss of independence and of control over all aspects of their lives, both at work and at home, which suggested to them that a growing tyranny existed, against which they must struggle to regain and retain their rights. Chartism expressed a strong resentment that the working class had been robbed of the fruits of its labour and was undergoing a diminution in its quality of life. It appeared to many workers that these grievances could be redressed only by their securing influence over the political system and the People's Charter was a means to that end. [2.]

Nineteenth-century commentators on Chartism regarded the role of the leaders a crucial factor in the 'failure' of Chartism. For many years the leaders' weaknesses were stressed mercilessly, and Feargus

O'Connor was made to bear the heaviest burden of responsibility. The leaders were pilloried for having provided inept and divided leadership and for encouraging violence among their desperate followers. Unagreed about what steps to take after the first petition was rejected, the leaders were placed into one of two clear-cut groups; one advocating 'physical' force and symbolised by O'Connor, the other 'moral' force and typified by William Lovett. While a useful tool for analysis, this division is misleading for it oversimplifies the differences between the leaders. [4.] That violence took place is undeniable and that armed risings were planned is clear; the Newport rising of 1839 tells us as much. [3.] However, the riots in Birmingham's Bull Ring in the same year were a response to police violence against the Chartists; disorder provoked by the authorities' endeavour to maintain public order. [8.] The Plug Plot disturbances of 1842 arose out of workers' resistance to wage cuts brought on by the decline of trade. Chartist leaders struggled to keep the strikers' eyes firmly fixed upon the restoration of 1840 wage rates; it was the strikers themselves who stressed the six points as the main condition for a return to work. [3.]

Women played a full part in the movement. Very few were aware of the ideas of Mary Wollstonecraft who had advocated, as early as 1792, the emancipation of women, through radical changes to their domestic role. The overwhelming majority accepted the man as the head of the family. The erosion of the traditional female role of wife and mother within the working-class family was deeply resented by women themselves. It had been eroded by the economic necessity of both women and children seeking employment for family survival. Far from seeing their liberation tied to the abolition of the domestic role, Chartist women sought to restore it. Many felt it had been destroyed by the new industrial practices. These had made women and children with no skills highly employable at low wages and for long hours in factories. This struggle for survival had robbed them of the chance to develop a full mother-child intimacy. It must not be forgotten, however, that Chartism was male-dominated and the restriction of female and child labour was regarded favourably by those who sought to drive up the wages of male workers by removing competition. In this respect Chartist men and women reflected the thinking of the age. The restoration of family life, and the woman's traditional role within it, was seen as one of the benefits which would flow from the winning of the six points. [6.]

Chartism was in part a response to the political events of the 1830s. Many felt a deep sense of betrayal towards the middle classes over the Reform Act of 1832. Working-class extra-parliamentary activities had been instrumental, if not indispensable, to its enactment. Yet it was an act which brought no improvement in the condition of the working class. On the contrary, the reformed parliament compounded the treachery by implementing measures such as the Poor Law Amendment

Act (1834), which worsened the condition of the poor, or the Municipal Corporations Act (1835), which weakened further the political influence of the labouring classes. The Factory Acts (1833), set beside these other reforms, were weak and ineffective and if enforced would have deprived families, who were already facing destitution, of essential income. The riotous opposition to the new Poor Law in particular raised consciousness among the masses that a conspiracy existed among the employing classes to impose further discipline over the lives of their employees. The answer to this was for the working classes to wrest political control from their masters by the achievement of the six points. [2.]

Chartism posed a threat to public order, which the government began to take seriously after the Newport rising of late 1839. The arrest, imprisonment, or even transportation of Chartists during 1839 and 1840 gave the government a respite only. The creation of the National Charter Association in 1840 and the release of the imprisoned leaders from 1841 onwards increased the threat as the trade depression deepened in 1842. A new petition was organised and rejected in that year and industrial unrest followed, such as the Plug Plots in which strikers removed the plugs from factory boilers to put out the fires so that work could not be continued by strikebreakers. [3.] The threat of disorder was met with ferocity; arrests, trials and imprisonments suppressed the agitation, which lost impetus as trade recovered.

These events brought out into the open a profound debate among the leadership about how best to proceed in the face of such committed opposition from the state. The 'physical force' argument had lost ground steadily in the face of the authorities' onslaught of 1839 and a number of ideas had been put forward, such as Lovett's plan for educating the masses through the Chartist organisation. Temperance, religion and co-operation with the middle classes through such organisations as the Complete Suffrage Union had all been urged before 1842. It was the lack of success in that year which encouraged the discussion of these ideas within the movement. [2.] This 'New Move' was condemned by O'Connor as Church Chartism, Teetotal Chartism, Knowledge Chartism and Household Suffrage Chartism. He feared that proceeding along any one of these routes would divert the masses from its single objective of the six points. After his release from prison in 1841 he had begun to increase his domination of the movement. He was reluctant to ally with the middle classes because he was convinced that the manufacturing classes were no friend of the workers. He pressed on with his Land Plan. By this, workers were to be settled upon smallholdings to render them self-sufficient and independent of the wage system. The scheme's collapse was due less to impracticality and financial mismanagement than to government hostility. [7.]

1848 was the year of revolutions in Europe and in Britain it saw the revival of the petition strategy. Fears of revolution abroad, stimulated by mass demonstration in support of a new petition, created an apprehension among the propertied classes that the destruction of the established order was imminent. Using large numbers of police the authorities controlled the London demonstration on Kennington Common and public order was maintained. [1.] Acting with party political purposes, the government had encouraged public fears of revolution in order to exaggerate its achievement in restoring order. The scorn poured upon this final petition created the impression that the events of 1848 constituted a fiasco. This was part of a government campaign which dealt Chartism a blow more mortal than that inflicted by the police and military during the unrest of that year. [8.]

The notion that Chartism had been a failure persisted among historians until the turn of this century. Then the perception grew that the failure to win the six points was an inadequate measure of Chartist success. It may be argued that they were unattainable in the context of the Chartist years. Perhaps success or failure judged in this way might be irrelevant to a movement whose very existence and survival was an achievement in itself. It was a movement of ordinary men and women undergoing intense suffering; the articulation of a conviction that they could move towards a future in which suffering was eradicated, if they could regain control over their lives by bringing about political changes. Through their activities and protest they placed two major questions upon the agenda of nineteenth century Britain – the Condition of England and the Constitutional Question. [10.]

The majority of sources used in this text have, in places, been slightly modified to preserve the sense for the modern reader.

# *The Chartist Years: A Sequence of Events*

*1836*

| | |
|---|---|
| June | Founding of the London Working Men's Association (LWMA). |
| August | National Radical Association of Scotland founded. |

*1837*

| | |
|---|---|
| January | LWMA drafts first petition to parliament. East London Democratic Association formed. |
| March | Beginning of LWMA missionary activity. |
| May | Revival of Birmingham Political Union (BPU). |
| May/June | Meeting of six radical MPs and six LWMA members produces a statement of the six points. |
| November | *Northern Star* first published in Leeds. |

*1838*

| | |
|---|---|
| April | Great Northern Union founded in Leeds. |
| May | Publication of the People's Charter. |
| August | Meeting in Birmingham adopts the Petition and the Charter. This marks the beginning of Chartism. |

*1839*

| | |
|---|---|
| February | General Convention meets in London. |
| May | Convention moves to Birmingham. |
| June | Petition to parliament with 1.2 million signatures. |
| July | Bull Ring Riots in Birmingham. Arrest of William Lovett. Convention returns to London. Petition rejected by 235 to 46. Convention calls for a 'Sacred Month'. |
| August | 'Sacred Month' called off. General Convention dissolved. |
| November | Newport rising. |
| December | Special Commission hears cases against Frost and others. |

*1840*

| | |
|---|---|
| January | Attempted risings in Yorkshire. |
| February/March | Chartist trials. |
| July | National Charter Association (NCA) founded in Manchester. Release of Lovett. Publication of *Chartism*. |

*1841*

| | |
|---|---|
| April | Lovett founds the National Association. |
| August | General Election – Peel new Conservative Prime Minister. |
| September | NCA initiates a new petition. |

*1842*

| | |
|---|---|
| January | Complete Suffrage Union (CSU) founded in Birmingham. |
| April | CSU Conference in Birmingham. NCA Convention meets in London; claims 50,000 members and 400 branches. |
| May | Second Chartist Petition (3.3 million signatures rejected by parliament – 287 votes to 49). |
| August/September | Industrial unrest; strikes against wage cuts. 'Plug' riots. People's Charter becomes strike aim. |
| October | Chartist trials begin. |

*1843*

| | |
|---|---|
| March | Trials of O'Connor and others at Lancaster. |
| September | NCA Convention in Birmingham accepts Land Plan. |

| | |
|---|---|
| *1844* | |
| April | NCA Convention in Manchester. |
| August | O'Connor debates the corn laws with Cobden at Northampton. |
| November | Publication of *Northern Star* in London. |
| *1845* | |
| April | NCA Convention in London. Land Co-operative Society formed. |
| October | Harney becomes editor of *Northern Star*. |
| December | Manchester conference agrees Land Plan. |
| *1846* | |
| March | Heronsgate acquired for 'O'Connorville'. |
| June | Repeal of the corn laws. |
| October | Lowbands bought for 'O'Connorville'. |
| December | Birmingham conference on the Land Plan. |
| *1847* | |
| May | 'O'Connorville' opened. |
| July | General election; Whigs returned under Lord John Russell. O'Connor elected as MP for Nottingham. |
| August | Land plan conference held at newly opened Lowbands. |
| *1848* | |
| February | Revolution in France. |
| March | Income tax demonstration in Trafalgar Square. Riots in Glasgow and London. Foundation of People's Charter Union. |
| April | Chartist Convention in London. Kennington Common meeting. Petition ridiculed in parliament. |
| May | National Assembly meets in London. Provisional executive elected. National Assembly dissolved. Riots in Bradford. Meetings and disorder in London. |
| June | Riots in London. Arrest of Ernest Jones in Manchester. Day of Protest (12th). |
| August | Planned insurrection in Britain. Select Committee reports on the Land Company published. |
| *1849* | |
| March | National Parliamentary and Financial Reform Association founded. |
| July | Great Dodford opened. |
| December | Chartist delegate conference held in London. |

*1850*

| | |
|---|---|
| January | O'Brien's National Reform League founded. Harney and London Democrats gain control of Chartist executive. |
| June | Harney's *Red Republican* published. |
| July | Jones released. |
| August | Harney leaves *Northern Star*. |

*1851*

| | |
|---|---|
| March | NCA Conference in London adopts social democratic policy. |
| May | Jones publishes *Notes to the People*. |
| August | Act to wind up Land Company passed. |
| December | Jones and Harney break with NCA separately. |

*1852*

| | |
|---|---|
| March | Last issue of *Northern Star*. |
| May | Jones begins *People's Paper*. Harney publishes *Star of Freedom*. Chartist conference at Manchester called by Jones. |
| June | O'Connor certified insane. |
| July | General election. Jones fights Halifax and is defeated. |

*1854*

| | |
|---|---|
| October | First part of Gammage's *History* published. |

*1855*

| | |
|---|---|
| August | Death of Feargus O'Connor. |

*1856*

| | |
|---|---|
| July | Frost returns from exile. |

*1858*

| | |
|---|---|
| February | Chartist conference votes to co-operate with the moderate liberal radicals. End of the Chartist Years. |

# 1 THE PEOPLE'S CHARTER

Between 1838 and 1858 the People's Charter became familiar to millions of working men and women. 'The Charter' or 'The Six Points' became shorthand terms for a programme of radical reform. It gave hope that something better than the prevailing 'Condition of England' was attainable. In the late 1830s the masses had concluded that the source of their suffering was their exclusion from politics. The Charter arose out of a meeting of the LWMA held at the Crown and Anchor Inn in London in 1837, and was written by William Lovett [4.A-J], one of the movement's early leaders [A & C].

The LWMA organised support for the Charter in the provinces, although such a course could be embarked upon only with great caution. The Corresponding Laws, which had been passed in the 1790s, were still in force. They had been enacted by a government fearful of the spread of revolutionary ideas from France. One of the organisations which had agitated for the 1832 Reform Act was the Birmingham Political Union (BPU). The Charter encouraged the revival of the BPU and it became an important part of the movement, initially led by middle-class radicals such as Thomas Attwood, who was more concerned with reform of the currency than with that of parliament. However, as organisation developed, support for the Charter and the petitioning of parliament became predominant and widespread [B-F].

A General Convention of delegates representing the movement was elected locally and called to meet in London in February 1839 to present the petition to parliament. In his description of the convention Lovett used the term 'physical force party', suggesting that it was divided; a point confirmed by R. G. Gammage, the author of the first history of Chartism. The rejection of the petition by parliament angered the Chartists, some of whom decided upon direct action. The best-documented rising took place in Newport, Monmouthshire, where an armed body of coal miners and iron workers marched upon the town [G-I].

In May of 1839 the convention moved to Birmingham, hoping to find greater security from government intimidation. A month later the Chartists met at the Bull Ring, where public meetings had been banned. They were attacked by police, whom the authorities had brought up by train from London specifically for the purpose. John Collins and William Lovett were arrested shortly after the riot because they had drawn up resolutions condemning the police action and they served a year in Warwick Gaol. During 1840 hundreds of Chartists were arrested, tried and imprisoned, including Feargus O'Connor [4.A-K] and James 'Bronterre' O'Brien [4.M,S-Hh], but agitation continued [J & K].

While the winning of the Charter remained the primary objective of the movement throughout the Chartist years, the three petitions, of 1839, 1842 and 1848, were significantly different from each other. That of 1839 concerned itself with the unrepresentative nature of parliament, while that of 1842 listed a number of other grievances. The 1842 petition also was rejected by parliament and a wave of strikes took place which became known as the 'Plug Plot'. The Chartist executive issued an address to the workers urging a general strike and this led to the arrest of many leaders including O'Connor. The strikes were called off after a week [L & M].

The failure of the two petitions provoked debate about future Chartist tactics and between 1840 and 1848 a number of different ideas emerged, labelled the 'New Move' [3.L-O]. O'Connor led the opposition to the 'New Move', asserting that the movement must not be diverted and must continue to focus upon the original Six Points, although he eventually adopted a change of tactics himself with his 'Land Plan' [7.D,H,K,L,P-X]. Revolution in France in February 1848 stimulated interest in a third petition and the movement returned to its old style of action. Nationwide unrest led to the foundation of the People's Charter Union and it resolved that a mass demonstration would march upon parliament in support of the new petition. The government banned the proposed march from Kennington Common to Westminster, and the Union could only submit and mask its impotence with a protest. Government repression and press ridicule of the petition were judged to have killed Chartism in 1848, but it struggled on until 1858 when the Six Points were reduced to two, as an immediate aim [N & P].

### A Lovett Describes the Creation of the People's Charter

In February 1837, our Association convened a public meeting for the purpose of petitioning Parliament. The prayer of that petition formed the nucleus of the far-famed *People's Charter*, which had its origin at this meeting. The public meeting was the most crowded and orderly I ever attended. All our resolutions were unanimously agreed to, and our petition signed by about three thousand persons.

From William Lovett: *My Life and Struggles* (1876)

### B LWMA Organisation of Support in the Provinces

A little previous to the inauguration of the movement for the Charter, the metropolitan Association had despatched its missionaries to the country for the purpose of forming provincial associations on the model of the original. The principal deputy engaged in these preliminary operations was Henry Hetherington. A fitter man could not have been selected, for his name was sufficient to procure the attendance of all the leading radical reformers.

From R.G. Gammage: *History of the Chartist Movement* (1854)

**C The People's Charter, 8 May 1838**

# The Six Points
OF THE
## PEOPLE'S
# CHARTER.

1. A VOTE for every man twenty-one years of age, of sound mind, and not undergoing punishment for crime.

2. THE BALLOT.—To protect the elector in the exercise of his vote.

3. No PROPERTY QUALIFICATION for Members of Parliament —thus enabling the constituencies to return the man of their choice, be he rich or poor.

4. PAYMENT OF MEMBERS, thus enabling an honest trades-man, working man, or other person, to serve a constituency, when taken from his business to attend to the interests of the country.

5. EQUAL CONSTITUENCIES, securing the same amount of representation for the same number of electors, instead of allowing small constituencies to swamp the votes of large ones.

6. ANNUAL PARLIAMENTS, thus presenting the most effectual check to bribery and intimidation, since though a constituency might be bought once in seven years (even with the ballot), no purse could buy a constituency (under a system of universal suffrage) in each ensuing twelvemonth; and since members, when elected for a year only, would not be able to defy and betray their constituents as now.

**D The LWMA Warns Local Associations to Remain within the Law**
We caution you not to form *branch associations*, because the Corresponding Act is still in force; nor to correspond *privately*, but publicly through the press. We invite one or more intelligent radical

reformers in every town to become *honorary* members of our association in London. Thus they can be made acquainted with all our proceedings in a *legal* manner. We intend to give increased publicity to our rules and objects, and will shortly give you further information through the columns of those newspapers which are disposed to assist us. We urge you to organise yourselves and resolve on victory! *With Union* everything will be accomplished; *without Union* nothing!

From William Lovett: *My Life and Struggles* (1876)

### E Winning the Approval of the BPU

Copies of this Address were forwarded to all working men's associations, radical associations, and political unions we were connected with; among others to the Birmingham Union, which we were anxious should declare in favour of universal suffrage. We sent down Henry Hetherington as a missionary to urge upon them the importance of the subject; but they, considering themselves pledged to the principles of the reform bill, remained for a long time staunch to that measure. However, previous to our issuing the above address, Mr. Attwood had begun to talk of the reform bill being 'nothing better than a witch's bantling,' and of the 'new set of borough-mongers being little better than the old'; and in the course of three months they came out nobly in favour of the suffrage.

From William Lovett: *My Life and Struggles* (1876)

### F Support for the Charter Becomes Widespread

The People's Charter was published on the 8th. of May 1838. The first public meeting it was submitted to was held in Glasgow on the 21st of May, when Thomas Attwood and the Council of the Birmingham Union visited Scotland. It very rapidly received the approval of numerous Associations in different parts of the country, and on the 6th. of August, by the men of Birmingham at one of the largest public meetings ever held in that town, our association having agreed to make their National Petition *the first petition for the Charter*.

From William Lovett: *My Life and Struggles* (1876)

### G The General Convention Meets in London

The General Convention of the Industrious Classes originated with the Birmingham Political Union, as did also the first National Petition. The delegates to this body were appointed by very large bodies of men. The Birmingham meeting was composed of 200,000, the Manchester meeting of 300,000, that of Glasgow of 150,000, of Newcastle 70,000, and other towns equally large in proportion to their population. The number of delegates composing the Convention was *fifty-three*, many of them representing several places, with the view to economy. Of this number three were magistrates, six newspaper editors, one clergyman of the Church of England, one Dissenting minister, and two doctors of medicine, the remainder being shopkeepers, tradesmen, and journeymen. They held their first meeting on Monday February 4th. 1839. On their assembling the Birmingham delegates proposed me as secretary, and though strongly opposed by some of the physical force party, I was eventually elected unanimously.

From William Lovett: *My Life and Struggles* (1876)

### H Gammage Confirms Lovett's View of a 'Split' Convention

The gentlemen of the Cobbet school were of the opinion that the body should be nothing more than a petition Convention. The vast majority were, however, of the contrary opinion. Moral and physical force men generally agreed that the people would expect something more. That after promises had been made, and hopes had been excited, there was no alternative but ulterior measures of some sort, in case the prayer of the petition was rejected. . .

Although the extreme section of the Convention received little countenance the majority were more disposed to the advocacy of physical force than otherwise. They were somewhat prompted to this course by the discontent, especially in the manufacturing districts, brought about by the most poignant distress and unrelieved by any hope of amelioration. That state of distress was frequently made the subject of discussion.

From R.G. Gammage: *History of the Chartist Movement* (1854)

### I The Newport Rising

Few of the reading public can have forgotten the insane attempt at insurrection made by the *Chartists* in Monmouthshire, when a body of misguided men, many thousand in number, led by three persons, *Frost, Williams,* and *Jones,* were dispersed by a small detachment of the 45th. regiment, amounting to only twenty-eight men, at the Westgate Inn, at Newport, in Monmouthshire.

The outbreak was to many a memorable one – or to too many a fatal one – to myself a fearful one; and, but for an irregularity in the legal proceedings, would have been to the three leaders, a terrible, and awful one – they were all three condemned to *Death*; and though their lives were spared, they were doomed (unless Her Majesty mercifully shorten the period) to drag out the remainder of their days in the penal settlements of South Australia.

From Barnabas Brough: *A Night with the Chartists* (1847)

### J The Chartist Response to the Police Attack in the Bull Ring

The morning after this brutal attack, a number of the working classes called at the Convention Rooms, and stated that they were anxious that some public expression of opinion should be made regarding the outrage, and some advice given to them as to what was best to be done respecting their right of public meeting. Feeling most strongly with them I drew up and proposed three resolutions, which were unanimously agreed to, and ordered to be printed. They were signed by myself and taken to the printer by John Collins.

The Resolutions Describe the Bull Ring Riot:—

'Wanton, flagrant and unjust outrage upon the people of Birmingham, by a bloodthirsty and unconstitutional force from London.' ADDING THAT: 'The people are the best judges of their right to meet in the Bullring or elsewhere', AND 'that there is no security for life, liberty, or property till the people have some control over the laws which they are called upon to obey.'

From William Lovett: *My Life and Struggles* (1876)

### K Despite Arrests and Imprisonments Agitation Continues

On Monday 20th. July 1840 a meeting of delegates assembled at Manchester to devise a plan for the placing of the body on a better footing. After several days' sitting, it was ultimately resolved to merge all the local bodies into one association to which they gave the name of the 'National Charter Association of Great Britain'.

From R.G. Gammage: *History of the Chartist Movement* (1854)

### L An Extract from the 1842 Petition

Thousands of people are dying from want; and your petitioners view with astonishment and alarm the ill provision made for the poor, the aged, and the infirm; and perceive with indignation, the determination of your honourable House to continue the Poor Law in operation . . .

Your petitioners would direct attention to the great disparity existing between the wages of the producing millions and the salaries of those whose usefulness ought to be questioned, where riches and luxury prevail amongst the rulers, and poverty and starvation amongst the ruled.

It is the undoubted constitutional right of the people to meet freely. Your petitioners complain that the right has been infringed, and 500 well disposed persons have been arrested, excessive bail demanded, tried by packed juries, sentenced to imprisonment, and treated as felons. An unconstitutional police is distributed all over the country, at enormous cost, to prevent the due exercise of the people's rights. The Poor Law Bastilles and the police stations have originated from the same cause, viz., the desire on the part of the irresponsible few to oppress and starve the many.

The hours of labour are protracted beyond the limits of human endurance, and the wages earned are inadequate to sustain the bodily strength and to supply those comforts which are so imperative after an excessive waste of physical energy. Your petitioners also direct attention to the starvation wages of the agricultural labourer.

From Hansard: *Parliamentary Debates* (1842)

### M The 'Plug Plot' (1842)

'The Plug Plot' began in reductions of wages by the Anti-Corn-Law manufacturers, who did not conceal their purpose of driving people to desperation to paralyse the Government. The people advanced at last, to a wild general strike, and drew the plugs so as to stop the works at the mills, and thus render labour impossible. The first meeting where the resolution was passed, 'that all labour should cease until the People's Charter became the law of the land', was held on Mottram Moor. In the course of a week the resolution had been passed in nearly all the great towns of Lancashire . . .

In Manchester troops and cavalry were going up and down the principal thoroughfares, accompanied by artillery drawn by horses. In the evening we held a meeting where O'Connor, the executive, and a number of delegates were present; it was evident they were filled with the desire of keeping the people from returning to their labour. They believed the time had come for trying to paralyse the Government. McDouall drew up an exciting and fiercely worded address to the working men of England, appealing to the God of Battles and urging a universal strike.

From Thomas Cooper: *The Life of Thomas Cooper* (1877)

### N A note from Richard Mayne (the Metropolitan Police Commissioner) to the Home Secretary (11.45am 10 April 1848)

I have seen Mr. O'Connor & communicated to him that the petition would be allowed to pass & every facility given for that, & its reaching the House of Commons, but no procession or assemblage of people would be permitted to cross the bridges.

Mr. O'Connor, gave me his word that the procession would not attempt to cross the Bridges. He added that the Petition should be sent in Cabs. There was considerable excitement amongst the people as Mr. O'Connor came to me. It was evidently supposed that he was taken into custody. He got on the top of a Cab to tell them he had received a friendly communication on which he was resolved to act.

From David Goodway: *London Chartism 1838–1848* (1982)

## O The Union Submits and Protests

The constitutional rights of Englishmen have been interfered with. On Monday a procession repaired from the Convention Hall to Kennington Common, where a quarter of a million were assembled. An intimation was then conveyed to us that no procession could be allowed to recross the river. We found that we were caught in a trap, that the bridges were closed against us, and that the vile proclamation of the government had been backed by warlike preparations on a scale so vast that it appeared as if a hostile armament of 200,000 men were about to besiege the metropolis. We felt constrained to embrace one of two alternatives – either to bring an unarmed people into collision with an armed authority or to leave the odium on the government of having prevented the exercise of an undoubted right. We chose the latter course.

From *Northern Star*, 15 April 1848

## P Benjamin Wilson on the Latter Days of Chartism

The Chartist movement had been neglected for some time in consequence of the broken health of Feargus O'Connor, and the *Northern Star* passing out of his hands; and Chartist leaders being imprisoned. Ernest Jones and his friends arranged a conference in Manchester in May 1852. It was not very well attended, as many towns had broken up their organisations. A few important towns were represented, and a number of letters of encouragement were received. A scheme of organisation was arranged, and Gammage, Fynland and Ernest Jones were appointed an Executive Committee. . .

Mr. Jones suggested that manhood suffrage and vote by ballot should be the future programme, and a conference held to consider the question. We decided to send a delegate to the conference to support Mr. Jones's suggestion. It met in London, Feb. 18th. 1858, upwards of 40 delegates being present. It was decided to agitate the country in favour of manhood suffrage and the ballot.

The agitation for the People's Charter had been in existence for nearly twenty years, but at length had come to an end. Our future programme was to be manhood suffrage and the ballot, in which we had the support of Cobden, Bright, Fox and a few other leading men.

From Benjamin Wilson: *The Struggles of An Old Chartist* (1887)

# Questions

1 What obstacles to working-class political action in the 1830s are illustrated by Sources A-F?                                    **(9 marks)**

**2** How far do Sources G-I confirm that there was a 'physical' and 'moral' force division within Chartism? **(7 marks)**

**3** What do Sources J and K indicate about the authorities' reaction to early Chartist agitation? **(7 marks)**

**4** Compare Sources L and M as indications of Chartist grievances. **(7 marks)**

**5** Using Sources N-P and your own knowledge assess the accuracy of the assumption that 'Chartism was dead by the end of 1848'. **(10 marks)**

# 2 CHARTIST IDEAS AND AIMS

The Six Points of the People's Charter are deeply rooted in English History. As early as the seventeenth century, a radical group, called the Levellers, had demanded a representative political system based upon universal suffrage and accountable to the people at large. These ideas were revived in the eighteenth century. Thomas Paine, a major political thinker late in the century, supported both the American Revolution in 1776 and the French Revolution of 1789. His ideas won him great affection and popularity among the nineteenth-century working classes in Britain, for his major work, *The Rights of Man*, had become one of the fundamental statements of radicalism. The Charter was based upon the concept that power derived from the people and this idea underlay the ideology of the American Revolution. It was reiterated in a declaration of the National Union of the Working Class (NUWC) written by Lovett and James Watson in 1831. Chartists held the same view [A-G].

Some Chartists looked back beyond the seventeenth century to the Norman Conquest in 1066. They embraced the 'Norman Yoke' theory, which asserted that the Anglo-Saxon people had held ancient rights and liberties of which they had been robbed by their Norman conquerors in order to enslave them. This group regarded the Charter as the means of retrieving their lost freedom. However, Chartism was not simply a backward looking movement; Feargus O'Connor often asserted that the Charter would modernise the political system, and George Julian Harney [4.L-R] viewed the Charter as a means of defending the working class against a conspiracy by the employers to impose tyranny over their employees. Largely a working-class organisation, the movement held firmly to the idea that only labour created wealth and that the labourers were being despoiled of the fruits of their labour. Many also had felt betrayed by the middle classes over the 1832 Reform Act, which had failed to enfranchise the working class. They saw the Charter as a means of redressing this grievance [H-M].

Although the Chartists united around the Six Points, there was a diversity of opinion among them about what the winning of the Charter might lead to. Some hoped it would lead to an entirely new social system, while others anticipated that it would produce a more representative government. Other groups expected that it would end their exclusion from the political system, which they were convinced was the cause of their impoverishment. Bronterre O'Brien thought that it would purge parliament of corruption and self-interest, which had led the House of Commons to be out of touch with the needs of society and to deal only in irrelevancies [N-Q].

It has been commonly held that working-class agitation was prompted by hard times [9.G-J]. The fall in living standards, much of which was induced by new industrial techniques, particularly the introduction of powered machinery into manufacturing, concerned many members of the movement. Although the impact of these changes was severe and the depression of 1837 intensified the misery, it was argued by contemporary Chartists that even between the periods of intense deprivation of the late 1830s and the 1840s Chartism continued to flourish, and the effect of the French Revolution of February 1848 upon the movement was a major stimulus to renewed activism. Chartists held a number of grievances which they hoped the Charter would enable them to redress, prominent among these were: the new Poor Law of 1834; taxation; and an extension of control over their lives through the new police forces being set up throughout the country [R-W].

## A The Third Agreement of the People, 1 May 1649

We the free People of England declare and publish to all the world, that we are agreed as followeth,

That the Supreme Authority of England and the Territories shall reside hence forward in a Representative of the people consisting of four hundred persons; in the choice of whom (according to natural right) all men of the age of one and twenty years and upward (not being servants, or receiving alms), shall have their voices; and be capable of being elected to that Supreme Trust.

From Don M. Wolfe: *Leveller Manifestoes of the Puritan Revolution* (1944)

## B Eighteenth-Century Radicals Held Similar Views

Our constitution is founded in injustice. Eight hundred individuals rule all accountable to none. Of these about 300 are born rulers, whether qualified or not. Of the others, a great many are said to be elected by a handful of beggars. Instead of the powers returning annually into the hands of the people the lengthening of parliament to the septennial has deprived them of six parts in seven of their power.

The people of England are the innumerable multitude, some have no representatives at all, and the rest are unequally represented.

Every man has what may be called property, and unalienable property. A life, a personal liberty, a character, a right to his earnings, a right to worship according to his conscience.

From James Burgh: *Political Disquisitions* (1774)

## C Thomas Paine on the Nature of Government

The laws of every country must be analogous to some common principle. In England, no parent or master, nor all the authority of parliament can bind or control the personal freedom even of an individual beyond the age of twenty-one years.

Every history of the creation agree[s] in establishing the unity of man; by which I mean, that all men are of *one degree* are born equal, and with an equal natural right.

Government ought to be open to improvement instead of which it has been monopolised from age to age, by the most ignorant and vicious of the human race. Need we any other proof of their wretched management, than the excess of debts and taxes with which every nation groans, and the quarrels into which they have precipitated the world.

From Thomas Paine: *The Rights of Man* (1791–2)

## D Working-Class Reverence and Affection for Paine

The object of this Association is to promote the Moral and Political condition of the Working Classes by disseminating the principles propagated by that great philosopher and redeemer of mankind, the Immortal 'THOMAS PAINE'.

The annual meeting of the Association be held on the 29th. January, being the anniversary of the death of that great Man, whose character and principles we duly appreciate, by a convivial supper on that occasion.

From the Prospectus of the East London Democratic Association, January 1837

## E Power Derives from the People

We hold these truths to be self-evident that all men are created equal, that they are endowed by their creator with certain unalienable Rights, that among these are Life, Liberty, and the pursuit of Happiness. – That to secure these rights, Governments are instituted among Men, deriving their just powers from the consent of the governed, – That whenever any Form of Government becomes destructive of these ends, it is the Right of the People to alter or abolish it, and to institute New Government.

From the *Declaration of the United States of America*, 4 July 1776

## F The Declaration of the NUWC, 1831

*We, the Working Classes of London*, declare –

1. All property (honestly acquired) to be sacred and inviolable.
2. That all men are born equally free, and have certain natural and unalienable rights.
3. That governments ought to be founded on those rights; and all

laws instituted for the *common benefit* in the protection . . . of *all the people*: and not for the particular advantage of any.

5.   That every man of the age of twenty-one years, of sound mind, and not tainted by crime, has a right to a free voice in determining the nature of the laws.

6.   The mode of voting should be *by ballot*; that intellectual fitness and moral worth, *and not property*, should be the qualification for representatives; and that the duration of Parliament should be but for *one year*.

From William J. Lynton: *James Watson, A Memoir* (1880)

## G The Chartists Held the Same View

From one principle may be deduced every true proposition relating to a democratic government: 'The people are the source of all power'.

Men first unite together for protection and mutual advantage; they feel the necessity of having some leader to control the vicious and reward the meritorious; they, therefore, *by the general voice, and for the general good*, invest one or more of their fellow-beings with superior authority; this alters not the source of that power; it must be found to spring originally from the people at large.

From *Northern Star*, 2 January 1841

## H The 'Norman Yoke' Theory

Not a few who are opposed to our possession of this right found their opposition on the ground that the claim is novel, and the experiment untried. However, the *existing* system is the innovation. The government of our Saxon ancestors, was conducted on the principle of universal suffrage, a testimony which is confirmed by the account given to Tacitus, of the customs of the country whence those ancestors emigrated to the British shores. Until historians of superior note shall venture to affirm to the contrary, we *might* enforce our claims upon the ground of ancient right.

From Kettering Radical Association: *Just Claims of the Working Classes* (1839)

## I Chartism – a Forward-Looking Movement. O'Connor in 1838

The old constitution was the constitution of tallow and wind. The people wanted the railroad constitution, the gas constitution, but they did not want Lord Melbourne and his tallow constitution; neither did they want Lord Melbourne and his fusty laws; what they wanted was a constitution of railroad genius, propelled by a steam power, and enlightened by the rays of gas, a legislature that had the power as well as the inclination to advance.

From R.G. Gammage: *A History of the Chartist Movement* (1854)

# PROCESSION

AND

# PUBLIC MEETING.

The Council of the National Charter Association have great pleasure in announcing that

# F. O'CONNOR

## ESQ., M. P.,

WILL VISIT LEICESTER

## ON MONDAY NEXT, MAY 8th,

### When he will deliver a LECTURE in the Amphitheatre,

## TO COMMENCE AT SEVEN O'CLOCK.

## Subjects:---THE CHARTER---THE LAND,
## And the best means to obtain them.

ADMISSION, to the Boxes & Stage, 6d; Pit 2d; Gallery 1d. Members free to the Gallery on producing their Cards.

It is intended to meet Mr. F. O'Connor in Procession at the Railway Station. The Chartists in Town and County—the Land Companies—the Various Trades—and all who are friendly to the enfranchisement of the millions—are respectfully invited to take a part in the proceedings.

The Members and Friends of the National Charter Association are requested to meet in the Market Place, at ONE O'CLOCK. The unfortunate Stone-Breakers, near the Old Workhouse, Humberstone Gate—each Body to arrange themselves six abreast, and proceed to the Market Place.

At a quarter before Two o'clock, 'the Procession thus formed, will proceed down Humberstone Gate, up Charles-street, Northampton-street, and Foxe's-street, to meet Mr. O'Connor by the down train, at fifteen minutes past Two. Upon a given Signal, the Procession will again move on, taking the following route, viz., London Road, Belvoir-street, Welford Road, Oxford-street, Friar Lane, Market-place, (entering by the Fish Market,) High-street, North Gate-street, Sanvy Gate, Church Gate, Belgrave Gate, Woodboy-street, Wharf-street, Rutland-street, Granby-street, and Humberstone Gate.

☞ On Friday evening next, at Eight o'clock, the Council will be happy to meet Deputations from the Trades and other Bodies, at the Association Rooms, Hill Street, to give further instructions.

The Members of the National Land Company, who intend to form a distinct part in the procession, are requested to meet at the Office, Church Gate, at One o'clock.

N. B. Persons wishing to become Members of the National Charter Association, may enrol their names and obtain cards of membership at Mr. H. Green's, Grocer, Rutland-street, or from

W. H. Burton, Printer, London Road.

**J Poster advertising a Chartist procession and Public meeting, 8 May 1838**

### K Harney on the Conspiracy to Tyrannise the Workers

I was for six months confined because I dared to give the working classes that untaxed knowledge which they have the right to enjoy. The Tyrants bound me, but they could not subdue me. They sent me away friendless and forlorn; but I return to Derby not as I departed. I come back to look the tyrants in the teeth, in the proud character of a leader of the people – as one of the chosen chieftains of the brave men of the north. We have met here today to demand our rights; we have assembled here to tell our tyrants that they shall tyrannise no longer.

From *The Operative*, 10 February 1839

### L Only Labour Creates Wealth

It is labour *alone which bestows value*. Every man has an undoubted right to all that his honest labour can procure him. When he thus appropriates the *fruits* of his labour, he commits no injustice upon any other human being; for he interferes with no other man's right of doing the same with the products of *his* labour.

From J.F. Bray: *Labour's Wrongs and Labour's Remedy* (1839)

### M The Betrayal of 1832

The masses were looking forward to an extension of political power, but were too easily turned aside. The middle class persuaded them to forego their extensive claims, in order to secure them ultimately. 'Aid us,' said they, 'in gaining the Reform Bill, and as soon as we are enfranchised we will make use of our power in assisting you to the attainment of your rights'. This was the promise invariably held out to the working class. A promise the more readily believed because at the time an idea pervaded their minds that the interests of the two classes were identical. It was conjectured therefore, that the one could have no purpose in deceiving the other. The wide disparity in the social position of the two classes was lost sight of altogether.

From R.G. Gammage: *A History of the Chartist Movement* (1854)

### N The Eradication of Social Problems through the Charter

Fellow-countrymen, when we contend of an equality of political rights, it is not in order to lop off an unjust tax or useless pension, or to get a transfer of wealth, power, or influence for a party; but to be able to probe our social evils to their source, and to apply effective remedies to prevent, instead of unjust laws to punish.

From *Address and Rules of the Working Men's Association*, June 1836

### O A More Utilitarian View
The foregoing rights [the Six Points] are claimed only as a means to an end which lies beyond them. That end is the establishment of such a mode of government as shall ensure the greatest possible happiness to all classes of the community.

From Kettering Radical Association: *Just Claims of the Working Classes* (1839)

### P London Shoemakers on their Exclusion from Politics
The great number of competitors in their trade, and the struggle for subsistence, which have led to a reduction in prices, are to be attributed to the monopolies, restrictions, and overburthening taxation, which exclusive and corrupt legislation have engendered. Though their trade union has to some extent been effective in protecting them against individual cupidity and injustice, they are satisfied that masters and men alike are the victims of those political causes.

From *Northern Star*, 27 August 1842

### Q Bronterre Considers Parliament
It is melancholy to witness the time of Parliament occupied with frivolous discussions. It would seem as though both factions had conspired to render the unrepresented millions as dead in public interest, as they are dead in law. Their whole talk is about trade or revenue, or appointments or privileges which affect only the members themselves, or the rich plundering faction of the country that elects them. To listen to their 'debates', one would suppose that the whole nation consisted of merchants, lawyers, placemen, and the like.

From *The London Mercury*, 19 February 1837

### R Wilson Reflects on Chartism in 1848
In this year [1848] flour was very dear, reaching the price of 5s. (.25p.) a stone (14 lbs.), whilst trade was also very bad. This was the time to make politicians, as the easiest way to get to an Englishman's brains is through his stomach. It was said by its enemies that Chartism was dead and buried and would never rise again. It was true there had been no meetings or processions but it was going on. Amongst combers, handloom weavers, and others politics was the chief topic. The *Northern Star* was their principal paper and it was a common practice, particularly in villages, to meet at friends' houses to read the paper and talk over political matters. We were only waiting for the time to come again. The French revolution [of 1848] gave the first impulse to this movement.

From Benjamin Wilson: *The Struggles of an Old Chartist* (1887)

### S Richard Marsden, of Preston, a Handloom Weaver
I am a handloom weaver, and can well recollect, when I could earn
thirty shillings [£1.50p.] per week – such was the case of the
handloom weaver in 1814 – and now the same amount of labour
performed would not produce seven shillings [35p]. In some fabrics
the loss was less than in others, but in none was the reduction less
than seven shillings in the pound.(Hear). However careful the weaver
might be there were mischances to which he, in common with all
mankind, was subject; but, unlike almost every other class who had
an opportunity of providing for them, they came upon him with
crushing power, because his wage had never been such as to allow
him to lay anything by with which to meet such casualties as sickness,
or unwilling idleness, a bad warp, or the thousand chances of a
fluctuating trade.

From *Northern Star*, 2 March 1839

### T An Address to the Middle Classes on Intolerable Deprivation
If you be not as blind, as hardened of heart as ever Pharaoh was of
old, you must perceive that a radical change must now very speedily
take place in the constitution of society which it is not in your power
to avert, though it is in your power to give it a peaceful character.

But it is not a question of courage it is a question of *necessity*;
watch your own child, as with tears it implores for a morsel; see the
eye of your own wife and sister grown dim with famine; feel hunger
tearing at your own vitals; then hear the shot-peal calling you to
death or freedom; opening to you a chance of escape from the hell
you endure, and you will rush into the shock of battle with a joy
bordering on madness.

*Northern Liberator*, 21 July 1839

### U Chartists Grievances – the New Poor Law of 1834
The operative looked upon the new enactment, as the breaking of the
last link in the chain of sympathy. Huge, prison-like workhouses had
risen serving to remind the poor of their coming doom. With scanty
wages, in many instances insufficient to support life in a tolerable,
state of comfort, there was nothing before them but misery in the
present, and the Bastile in the future, in which they were to be
immured when the rich oppressor no longer required their services.

From R.G. Gammage: *A History of the Chartist Movement* (1854)

### V Chartist Grievances – Taxation
You take three-fourths of their earnings by your complicated system
of taxation, and by your monopolies force them into unequal

competition with other nations, you have exhibited a contempt for their complaints in your profligate and lavish expenditure at home and abroad, and by a selfish pertinacity in favour of the monopolies you have created for your own especial interests or those of your party.

From the 1842 Chartist Remonstrance to the House of Commons. William Lovett: *My Life and Struggles* (1876)

## W Chartist Grievances – Increased Policing

About the same time the police system was coming into active operation. The large towns were first burdened with this new force, but it was afterwards extended to the smaller towns and villages. This gave a considerable shock to the old English feelings of the people, who saw in the various schemes afloat a tendency to centralisation which aims at the abolition of local authority.

From R.G. Gammage: *A History of the Chartist Movement* (1854)

# Questions

1 Using Sources A-E examine the origins of the Six Points.   **(7 marks)**

2 What do Sources F and G indicate about the Chartist view of the nature of government?   **(8 marks)**

3 To what extent do Sources H, I, K, L and M suggest that Chartists were concerned only with regaining lost rights?   **(7 marks)**

4 Does the evidence in Sources N-Q support or challenge the view that Chartism was a divided movement?   **(8 marks)**

5 From your own knowledge and the evidence in Sources V-W, discuss the claim that Chartism was 'knife and fork question'.   **(10 marks)**

# 3 CHARTIST STRATEGIES AND TACTICS

The People's Charter was a demand for democracy and the Chartists sought to introduce democratic processes into the conduct of their own affairs. Bronterre O'Brien was delighted with the democratic style of the meeting which approved the Charter in 1837. An important form of Chartist activity was the open-air mass meeting and it was at such meetings that the delegates for the General Convention were elected in February 1839. The convention originally was intended to present the petition to parliament, but inevitably it turned its attention to considering what action to take, should the petition be rejected. One possibility was an 'Election Plan' devised by O'Brien [D]. This proposed that Chartists should present themselves at the hustings, which preceded parliamentary elections. The hustings differed from the ballot in that anyone present could vote in a show of hands after the various speakers had addressed the crowd. O'Brien planned that the victors in the show of hands should march upon parliament and occupy it as the true representatives of the people. In May the Convention, which had moved to Birmingham, discussed what to do if parliament rejected the petition. Ways to pressurise the government were drawn up and these 'Ulterior Measures' were submitted, in question form, for approval to simultaneous mass meetings of Chartists throughout the country [A-E].

Despite the movement's devotion to democracy, outbreaks of violence frequently occurred. Some occasions were direct responses to brutality by the authorities, others took the form of industrial action. Outright rebellion was attempted, but violence in general tended to be inherent in the political activity of the day. Less vigorous forms of action included the boycott of shops whose proprietors were not Chartist sympathisers [H-K].

The failures of 1839 and the imprisonment of over 500 Chartists led to a reappraisal of the movement's strategy which became known as the 'New Move'. In gaol Lovett and John Collins wrote *Chartism*, a book which urged the education of the masses as the road to their emancipation, and spelt out in detail how this could be achieved. A second aspect of the 'New Move' is to be found in the growing support for the Temperance movement among Chartists. This presented organisational problems as many Chartist meetings were held in alehouses. A third development was Christian Chartism. This was an effort to make the movement more 'respectable' by founding Chartist churches, while at the same time freeing the people from the influence of established religion [L-N].

The 'New Move' met with strong opposition. It was felt that new strategies would distract the masses from the unifying objective of the Six Points. O'Connor condemned it as 'Knowledge Chartism, Teetotal Chartism, Christian Chartism, and Household Suffrage Chartism', and claimed that it betrayed the Charter because it assumed that the workers could be enfranchised only when they reached certain educational, moral or religious standards. An alliance with the middle classes was considered as a possible strategy by some Chartists. Middle-class men, such as Thomas Attwood of Birmingham, had left the movement because of the violent tone of the 1839 convention. The Anti-Corn Law League (ACLL) and Joseph Sturge's Complete Suffrage Union (CSU) which paradoxically campaigned for household suffrage only, presented two such opportunities for class co-operation, but class antagonism was too deep. O'Connor's opposition to the 'New Move' and the middle-class initiatives stemmed from a desire to keep Chartism firmly wedded to the original Six Points. He was less than confident in the strategy of mass petitions and during the 1840s he devised his Land Plan [7.D-H,K,L,P-X]. However, it was to their original strategy that the Chartists returned in their final year as a mass movement [1.N,O]. A monster petition to parliament was backed by a huge demonstration on Kennington Common during the Easter weekend of 1848 [O-Q].

## A Bronterre on the Crown and Anchor Meeting, February 1837

Never was it my good fortune to witness so brilliant a display of democracy as that which shone forth at the Crown and Anchor. I often despaired of Radicalism before; I will never despair again.

Four thousand were present. The immense room was crowded to overflowing, several hundreds stood outside on the corridor and the stairs. The meeting was convened to petition for a reform of Parliament based on the five cardinal points of Radicalism.

The . . . proceedings were originated, conducted, and concluded, by working men in a style which would have done credit to any assembly in the world.

From *The London Mercury,* 4 March 1837

## B An Open-Air Mass Meeting in Nottingham in 1842

The Market-place was thronged with people, while from the different villages round, and from distant places, processions kept coming in. The procession was an extremely good one. First came a man mounted on a grey horse, with the Chartist colours (green) tied over it. Next came four beautiful green wreaths, suspended from an upright pole with cross-bars, and then a large green silk flag bearing the inscription [of the Six Points and] 'Our cause is just'. Beside it was a plain pink flag. A band of music was here stationed. Next came a number of small flags borne by children, and then a large green flag. Two small flags, green and pink, with 'Feargus O'Connor' on them. Likenesses of Oastler, O'Connor and Emmet mounted on the tops of poles, presented a gay appearance.

Next came another band of music, and the carriage and four greys, containing O'Connor. A number of flags and flys drawn by single horses, full of women and men, followed. Next came a large banner with the boot-makers' arms on it – a very valuable and choice flag. The next flag bore the inscription, 'They have set up Kings, but not by me – God is our King – him I will obey'. Next the inscription, 'We have set our lives upon the cast, and we will stand by the hazard of the die'. A band of music followed. A large red flag, having on it 'Freedom to the whole Family of Man,' – a pink flag, 'Union is Strength' – a green flag with 'The Charter' and 'No Surrender' – a large flag with 'Ilkeston National Association' – a white flag with 'No Surrender' upon it and the Heanor band closed the procession.

From *Nottinghamshire Review*, 26 February 1842

### C The Election of Delegates to the 1839 Convention
It was now determined that instead of local petitions there should be one general or national petition – each district to send in signatures to it, and elect representatives to a national convention to meet in London to present this petition to the House of Commons and urge its support on the members.

During the autumn of 1838 a public meeting was held in the open air to elect the delegates for the Newcastle district. The different associations of the district had been consulted as to the number of members to be elected, and the persons who they would put in nomination. The choice fell on Dr. John Taylor, Julian Harney, along with myself. When the meeting assembled, which was numerously attended, we were elected unanimously.

From Robert Lowery: *Passages in the Life of a Temperance Lecturer* (1857)

### D Bronterre on the 'Hustings Plan'
Would not Oastler* have the show of hands at Huddersfield? Would not Feargus O'Connor have ten to one almost anywhere? Is there one of the metropolitan boroughs in which two Chartists would not have an overwhelming majority of hands? I tell you that 400 delegates elected by an average majority of five to one, would be the real *bona fide* representatives of the country.

[* Richard Oastler was a factory reformer from Yorkshire and a fiery anti-Poor Law agitator. He was unenthusiastic about universal suffrage, and was sometimes described as a Tory-reformer.]

From Alfred Plummer *Bronterre* (1971)

### E Ulterior Measures
1. Whether Chartists will withdraw all sums of money they may have placed in savings banks etc., and convert their paper money into gold and silver?
2. Whether, *if the convention shall determine that a sacred month will be necessary*, they will abstain from their labours during that period, as well from the use of intoxicating drinks?
3. Whether they would refuse payment of rent, rates and taxes?
4. Whether they have prepared themselves with the arms of freemen to defend the laws and constitutional privileges their ancestors bequeathed to them?
5. Whether they will support Chartist candidates at the General Election?
6. Whether they will deal exclusively with shopkeepers known to be Chartists?
7. Whether they will resist all counter and rival agitations?
8. Whether they will refuse to read hostile newspapers?

From *The Charter*, 19 May 1839

### F Violence in the Bull Ring in May 1839, [1.J,K]
The people indulged in loud shouts, and commenced singing the Chartist anthem. 'Fall tyrants, fall!' which was followed by deafening cheers. There arose a loud cry of 'Holloway! Holloway!' and the people immediately marched to Holloway Head, where they swore vengeance against the metropolitan police, then to St. Thomas's church, tearing down the pallisades and making them into arms. Seventy feet of railing were torn down, and the rails made into weapons. The large and strong iron gates were wrested off, and the massive pillars on which the gates swung were twisted from their positions, giving evidence of the power of even an unarmed people, when roused to fury by injustice. Armed they were rushing to the scene of conflict, when they were met by Drs. Taylor and M'Douall, who with the utmost difficulty persuaded them to throw down their arms.

From R.G. Gammage: *A History of the Chartist Movement* (1854)

NOT SO *VERY* UNREASONABLE!!! EH?"

'*John.* "My Mistress says she hopes you won't call a Meeting of her Creditors; but if you will leave your Bill in the usual way, it shall be properly attended to."

**G** *Punch* cartoon: Not so very unreasonable !!! Eh?

## H The Debate on the 'Sacred Month'

The petition had now been presented – the House of Commons was averse to its prayer, and from this time began the difficulties of the convention. The 'sacred month' was an idea which had originated with the Birmingham men. Whatever might have been meant by it at first, it meant in the people's minds the chances of a physical contest that by retiring from labour they would so derange the whole country that the authorities would endeavour to coerce them back, and they would resist the authorities unless their rights were conceded, and thus bring the struggle to an issue. Seeing that if the Convention recommended the sacred month it would assuredly lead the people wrong and most likely cause breaches of the peace, I succeeded in getting the question discussed with closed doors. There was evidently a conviction that a national holiday could not be kept, but a total lack of courage among the leading men to say so. The Convention passed a resolution stating what they had done to attain the Charter, and left it to the people to decide whether they should keep the sacred month or not.

From Robert Lowery: *Passages in the Life of a Temperance Lecturer* (1857)

## I The Monmouth Rising. Evidence of George Hodge

I am a collier, I live near the Blackwood. I was at home on Sunday the 3rd. of November. A number of men from 7 to 10 came to my house. They were armed. A gun or two and a pike or two. At the Coach and Horses I saw Frost. There was a considerable number of men present. Frost said Zephania Williams was to meet them with 5,000 men. Jones of Pontypool, was to meet them with about 2,000. Some of the men made the remark of what was the good of going there without arms? Someone made the answer that there were plenty of guns, bayonets and ammunition there. I ran up to Frost and said to him 'In the name of God what are you going to do? Are you going to attack any place?' and he said 'Yes; to attack Newport, and to take it.' He also said he would blow down the bridge and stop the Welsh mail from proceeding to Birmingham. The delegates were then to be in waiting an hour and a half after time, and if the mail did not arrive by that time they would attack Birmingham and spread all through the North of England.

From *The Charter*, 17 November 1839

## J Strong-arm Tactics – An ACLL Meeting Ends in Chaos

Shouts of 'Go on the hustings, White', arose from all parts of the hall. White proceeded towards the hustings, and Ridley, Rouse, and other active Chartists moved forward at the same time. This was the signal for a general row. The men on the platform rising in a body, clenching their fists, and placing themselves in a fighting attitude, headed by the parson. Ruffy Ridley being the first to ascend the hustings, was unceremoniously knocked off by the fighting parson, another of the gentry at the same time striking at White, but having missed, White seized him by the collar and threw him into the body of the meeting, and the Chartist body proceeded at once to contest the platform hand to hand, and in five seconds put the whole troop of well-fed middlemen to the rout.

From *Northern Star*, 6 May 1843

### K A Less Vigorous Form of Chartist Action – 'Exclusive Dealing'

The middle-class shop keepers promised that if we assisted to get them the Reform Bill they would get us the vote; they have broken their pledge. What is our remedy against this evil? – Exclusive dealing. We have made them and we can unmake them. Our pennies make their pounds. If we cease to deal with them they will become poor, and lose their votes. They will then feel the evils they now inflict upon us and cry out for universal suffrage. Thus, while ceasing to spend our money in the shops of our enemies, we have destroyed their power.

From Robert Lowery: *Address on the System of Exclusive Dealing* (1839)

### L The 'New Move' – Chartist Education

The reflecting portion of our brethren are beginning to perceive the great necessity for this intellectual and moral preparation; – not as set forth by those 'educationists' who seek to spread their own notions, or those who seek to train up the youthful to be submissive admirers of 'things as they are'; but for establishing such a system as shall make our country intellectually great, politically free, and socially happy . . .

There is evil to be apprehended from placing the education of our children in the hands of any government. It becomes one of the most important duties of the working and middle classes to establish a just and liberal system of education, lest the power of educating their own children be taken from them by the arbitrary act of a corrupt and exclusive government.

From William Lovett and John Collins: *Chartism* (1840)

### M The 'New Move' – Chartism and Temperance

In order to secure proper places of meeting we proposed a plan for the erecting of *Public Halls for the People* in every district of the kingdom; by which our working-class brethren might be taken out of the contaminating influences of public houses and beer-shops where many of their meetings are held, in which their passions are inflamed, their reason drowned, their families pauperised, and themselves socially degraded and politically enslaved.

From William Lovett: *My Life and Struggles* (1876)

## N The 'New Move' – Christian Chartism

I am delighted with your reference to the progress of Chartist Christianity against the long-faced hypocritical pharisees whose religion consists in preaching slavery to the poor under the name of humility, and dutiful submission to the 'powers that be', which are 'ordained by God', although the sleek vagabonds well know that, without the devil such 'powers' would never have been heard of. By all means get rid of the 'black slugs'; by all means protect the consciences and the cabbages of the poor from the 'black slugs'.

From *Northern Star*, 2 January 1841. Letter from O'Neil – Birmingham Christian Chartist to McRae – Scottish Chartist preacher and schoolmaster

## O O'Connor on the 'New Move'

I am anxious to see every Chartist a good Christian, a good neighbour and a good friend. I am desirous of seeing every Chartist sober, industrious, honest full of knowledge and filling houses. I believe that a hypocritical use of those inestimable blessings will impede, or altogether destroy their possession . . .

My friends get your Charter, and I will answer for the religion, sobriety, knowledge, and house and a bit of land into the bargain.

From *Northern Star*, 3 April 1841

## P J.F. Bray on Class Animosity

The gain of the employer will never cease to be the loss of the employed – until the exchanges between the parties are equal; and exchanges can never be equal while society is divided into capitalists and producers – the last living upon their labour and the first bloating upon the profit of that labour. Establish whatever form of government we will, we may talk of morality and brotherly love, no reciprocity can exist where there are unequal exchanges.

Where equal exchanges are maintained, the gain of one man cannot be the loss of another; for every exchange is then simply a *transfer*, and not a *sacrifice* of labour and wealth.

From J.F. Bray: *Labour's Wrongs and Labour's Remedy* (1839)

## Q Gammage on the CSU

In 1842, a fresh source of disunion arose in the Chartist ranks. Joseph Sturge, who had abandoned the Anti-Corn Law movement on account of the want of principle evinced by its leaders put forth a declaration on the right of every man to the franchise. This called upon the friends of parliamentary reform to sign, and to meet him in conference at Birmingham, to devise the best means of forwarding their object. A number of the Chartists looked with favour on this movement. But however favourable were the Chartists to the efforts of Sturge, O'Connor and his party denounced those efforts.

From R.G. Gammage: *A History of the Chartist Movement* (1854).

# Questions

**1** What evidence in Sources A, B, C and D indicates that the Chartists were not only supporters of democracy but also practised it?

**(9 marks)**

**2** How far do Sources E and K suggest that Chartists were anxious to avoid violence? **(7 marks)**

**3** With reference to Sources L-N explain what is understood by the term 'the New Move'. **(7 marks)**

**4** Why, according to the evidence in Source O, did O'Connor oppose the 'New Move'? **(7 marks)**

**5** Using Sources P and Q and your own knowledge assess the contention that Chartism was a class movement. **(10 marks)**

# 4 CHARTIST LEADERS

Many men were considered to be 'Chartist Leaders', but some were of only local importance with no claim to national status [5.A & B]. Four will be studied in this chapter: Feargus O'Connor, who dominated the movement, and William Lovett, who wrote the original Charter, are obvious choices. The other two are George Julian Harney and James 'Bronterre' O'Brien. Harney represented the left wing of the leadership, and moved towards international socialism in the late 1840s; O'Brien was a devotee of the French Revolution of 1789, and might be called the theorist of the movement. These men played a vital part in leading the movement nationally.

O'Connor and Lovett emerged from London radicalism in the 1830s. O'Connor was born in Ireland in 1796, to parents of the lesser gentry. A lawyer, he came to London as MP for Cork in the first Reformed Parliament. Lovett's parents were Cornish artisans. He moved to London in 1821 at the age of twenty-one and established himself as a cabinet-maker. By 1830 he was well-known in the radical and working-class movements, and he took an active part in the campaign for an unstamped press [8.B]. In personality the two men were very different; O'Connor a flamboyant orator, Lovett a dedicated administrator, who thought O'Connor's leadership was misguided and came to resent the Irishman's domination of Chartism. Lovett was involved in the LWMA; while O'Connor founded the Marylebone Radical Association and in 1837 launched the *Northern Star*. A dislike festered between the two which erupted when O'Connor criticised the LWMA and Lovett responded with a bitter personal attack. This mutual dislike obscured an ideological difference. Lovett wanted to raise the educational and moral standards of the working class to make them fit to enter politics. O'Connor, while aware of the condition of the masses, saw the franchise as every man's right, regardless of education or morality. Lovett was convinced that O'Connor was foremost among those in the 1839 convention who had misled the masses. He detested disorder, and regretted his own role in encouraging 'Ulterior Measures'. O'Connor doubted the effectiveness of the LWMA's strategy and wrote ironically of Lovett's desire to create a 'respectable' working class [A-F].

O'Connor has been labelled a 'physical force' Chartist. It might be more accurately claimed that he did not advocate violence as a means of winning the Charter, but supported the right to armed self-defence against the authorities. It is true, however, that he predicted violence if the Charter was rejected by the government. His reputation as a man of violence came in part from his oratorical style; he needed to enthuse his audience and consequently appeared to be ambiguous on the subject of violence. Frequently he used extremely forceful language to express quite moderate aims. His reputation was damaged by adverse criticism, sometimes unjustified [10.Q-V]; Gammage, for example, perceived O'Connor as Lovett's enemy and depicted the former as domineering rather than dominant [G-K].

George Julian Harney was born in 1817 to working-class parents in Deptford, south London. He took a job in 1831 on the *Poor Man's Guardian*, which involved him in the unstamped press campaign [8.B] and he served three prison terms on this account. He learned of the French Revolution of 1789 from O'Brien, the newspaper's editor. In 1837 he formed the East London Democratic Association [2.D], which was opposed to and by the LWMA. His revolutionary fervour led him to use violent imagery which was too militant for Lovett, and like O'Connor he too was identified as a 'physical force' Chartist. In 1839 he echoed Feargus, demanding universal suffrage as a right, and urging violence only as a last resort. Harney's view of the use of force was a considered one. When he opposed the extension of the 'Plug Plot' strikes at the 1842 Convention, Thomas Cooper suggested that he had joined the 'moral force' party. In Sheffield later in the year Julian gave a clearer view of why he opposed the strikes' extension. By refusing to lead unarmed strikers against armed troops, he dissuaded a mass meeting from joining in the industrial stoppages. In 1843 he replaced O'Brien as editor of the *Northern Star*, which by then had moved to London. There he formed links with international socialists such as Karl Marx and Friedrich Engels. Under this influence he began to view the British working class as part of an international proletariat engaged in class struggle [L-R].

James 'Bronterre' O'Brien was born in Ireland in 1805, the son of an impoverished merchant. Well-educated, he came to London in 1829 with the intention of practising law. He entered the radical movement almost at once and became involved in the unstamped press campaign. He was an authority on the French Revolution of 1789, and it was his hope that the unrepresented would ultimately seize political power, for he viewed parliament with little more than contempt [3.D]. He recommended the working classes to arm themselves, but for the purpose of self-defence against government repression only, for he saw violence as self-defeating. In a speech which he made in Newcastle-upon-Tyne in 1839 he advocated arming for self-protection and it was the cause of his arrest, trial and acquittal. However, a similar prosecution against him was successful in Liverpool and he was imprisoned in 1840. Released from prison in 1841, he became less active in the movement; he disliked the newly formed National Charter Association (NCA), although he continued to support Chartism through his journalism. He split with O'Connor over Sturge's CSU [3.Q] and the Irishmen's dispute worsened over the land question [7.H-M]. In 1848 he was on the margins of the movement and although he urged the Chartist convention to avoid violence, he was not present at the Kennington Common rally. By this time he had developed a marxist view of the working class. In December 1849 he formed the National Reform League (NRL), not so much to rival Chartism as to give it direction. The NRL advocated a number of socialist principles, upon which a reconstituted political system should be based. It is worth noting that, taken with his opinion of private property, they appear to follow the ideas of Robert Owen rather than those of Karl Marx. O'Brien was always a Chartist; after 1850 he resumed lecturing for the Charter and opposed anything which might split the movement or divert it from its primary objective of the Six Points [S-Hh].

### A A Non-Partisan View of the Leaders

Working men feel an ardent devotion to Lovett and O'Brien, but while they appreciate the stirling honesty, the active intelligence, the indomitable perseverance, the glorious enthusiasm which distinguish the individuals in the front of the army – in no one name do they discern qualities so commanding in attracting an unswerving attachment, as in their brave O'Connor.

From *Midland Counties Illuminator*, 17 April 1841

### B Lovett Criticises O'Connor

You have dubbed yourself 'the missionary of all the Radicals of London'. You carry your fame about with you; you are the great 'I AM' of politics – Feargus O'Connor. Could self-idolatry do more, without blushing? You would have it that we have been neglectful of the working men, because we choose another path from yours. But time will show who are their real friends; whether they are 'the leaders of the people' who make furious appeals to their passions or those who seek to unite them upon principles of knowledge and temperance, and the management of their own affairs.

From William Lovett: *My Life and Struggles* (1876)

### C Lovett's View of the Working Classes

The working classes were always being swayed in opinion by the *idol* of their choice, and were divided when some popular breath had blown that *idol* from its pedestal. In fact the masses were taught to look up to *great men* rather than to great principles. We wished to establish a political school of self-instruction and form a sound and healthful opinion throughout the country. We felt that no political morality could be formed so long as our fellow-workmen continued to croak over their grievances with maudlin brains, and appetites for drink amid the fumes of the tap-room.

From William Lovett: *My Life and Struggles* (1876)

### D O'Connor Sees Universal Suffrage as a Right
It appears to me to be absolutely necessary for the people to have control over the man who has dominion over his life, his labour and his property. (Cheers.) The suffrage, therefore, is the question after all, and I am determined, wherever I meet you, be the subject under consideration what it may, to bring forward the question of Universal Suffrage.

From *Leeds Times*, 20 May 1837

### E Lovett's Disavowal of Violence
He [O'Connor] subsequently and on several occasions endeavoured to persuade his dupes that I was the concoctor of the violent measure, although himself and his disciples were the first to talk of arming, of the run on the banks, and the *sacred month*. I mention these facts in no way to disclaim the hand I had in it, although I believe that I did an act of folly in being a party to *some of its provisions*, but I sacrificed much in that convention for the sake of union and I still believe that if I had not been imprisoned I could have prevented many of the outbreaks and follies that occurred.

From William Lovett: *My Life and Struggles* (1876)

### F O'Connor Mocks Lovett and the LWMA
It is strange that Lovett & co, who profess that *working men should depend on themselves alone* are always found unable to take any public step, except under the express patronage of members of Parliament. For men who are anxious to shake off the degrading dependence of labourers on the wealthy classes, the managers of the WMA look uncommonly comfortable, as they sit cheek by jowl, at public meetings, with the Malthusian owners of ten thousand a year.

From *London Mercury*, 30 April 1837

### G O'Connor on Violence
The constitution told us that every man had a right to have a musket over his door, because it might be necessary to use it in his own defence – (Loud cheers.) He did not preach physical force; he had been preaching moral power for five years – what grievances they ought to bear – what amount of endurance they ought to suffer. Physical force would come as soon as the cup of suffering was

overflowing; and he believed that the cup of suffering was now very nearly overflowing.

From *Manchester and Salford Advertiser*, 10 February 1838

**H O'Connor at Kersal Moor, Near Manchester, (September 1838)**
Universal suffrage . . . was 'My night dream, my morning thought'. I have stood by this all along. Is it because I am a man of blood? No. I look upon universal suffrage as the only principle which can stop the flowing of human blood. You will never be represented until every man is intrusted with that which nature has imprinted on the breast of every man, namely the power of self-defence, as implied in the vote of every individual; and, when I have counselled you, that you had not tried your power to its full bearing, I referred to your moral power. Now here is moral power with a vengeance, which will be turned ere long, in spite of me, or of the most wise counsellors of the age, into physical force, because the people know that they have borne oppression too long and too tamely. You are united as one man; and if you now stop, it will be your own fault. No man can have heard the speeches today without knowing success is certain. Let us go on with our moral force. I have commenced the battle of the suffrage with you, and you are the forces with which I will fight this battle, even to the death. (Cheers.)

From *Northern Star*, 29 September 1839

**I A Yorkshire Chartist Notes His Impact Upon Audiences**
His figure was tall and well-proportioned, and his bearing aristocratic. He wore a blue frock-coat and buff waistcoat, and rings on the fingers of each hand. In a graceful manner and in emphatic language, he told the Radicals of Barnsley that he would henceforth devote his whole life to promote the well-being of the working classes. The language of O'Connor, to ears accustomed to little else than the Barnsley dialect spoken by pale-faced weavers and swart cobblers, sounded like rich music.

From *Barnsley Times*, May 1882

**J Gammage's View of Lovett v. O'Connor**
The *Northern Star* contained from time to time letters and articles denouncing all as traitors who favoured the plan of Lovett and Collins. O'Connor wrote a letter on 'Knowledge Chartism, Teetotal Chartism, and Christian Chartism,' in which he emphatically denounced all three as organised systems; but against the first his letter was more especially directed.

From R.G. Gammage: *A History of the Chartist Movement* (1854)

PUNCH'S PENCILLINGS.—Nº. LI.

THE MODERN MILO.

*Vide*—"The Life and Times of Feargus O'Connor."

K *Punch* cartoon: The modern Milo

### L Harney Prefers O'Connor

A popular chief should be possessed of a magnificent bodily appearance, an iron frame, eloquence. I have none of these. O'Connor has them all. A popular leader should possess great animal courage, contempt of pain and death, and be not ignorant of military arms and science. From a knowledge of all the men in the Chartist movement, I am convinced that was O'Connor thrown overboard, we might go further and fare worse.

From F.G. & R.M. Black: *The Harney Papers* (1969)

### M Harney the Revolutionary

Rather than live as we now live I will call upon my countrymen to weave no more for their tyrants but their winding sheets – to dig no more but their graves. Three months will bring about the change we seek; and 1839 shall be as memorable in the annals of England as 1793 is in the annals of France.

From *The London Dispatch*, 13 January 1839

### N Harney's Perception of Universal Suffrage and Force

Our country may be compared to a bedstead full of Aristocratic and Shopocratic bugs. To [those] who say we wish to destroy property, I answer that we will not destroy the bedstead, but *we will annihilate the bugs*. We have met to demand our rights. We demand Universal Suffrage, because that will bring universal happiness or our tyrants shall find that we will have universal misery.) (Cheers.) Our oppressors shall share the misery. (Cheers.) Universal Suffrage will bring freedom to our country and happiness to our homesteads; it will give us bread, and beef, and beer. What is it that we want? Not to destroy property and take life, but to preserve our own lives, and to protect our own property – viz, our labour. We are for Peace, Law and Order; but if our tyrants shall violate the law we shall defend the few remaining rights left us by our fathers. We must have justice speedily; peaceably if we can, forcibly if we must. (Loud Cheers).

From *Northern Star*, 9 February 1839

### O Thomas Cooper Describes Harney at the 1842 Convention

Nothing caused so much amazement in the Conference as the speech of Harney the renowned invoker of the spirits of Marat, Danton and Robespierre, in the old Convention times! – Julian, the notorious advocate of physical force at all times!

'What! Julian turned "moral-force humbug"! – what will happen next?' was said by the advocates of the strike. A more sincere or honest man than Julian, perhaps, never existed.

From Thomas Cooper: *The Life of Thomas Cooper* (1872)

### P Harney to the Sheffield Workers during the Plug Plot of 1842

Are you ready to fight the soldiers? You may say that this is not the question but I tell you that it would be the question. I do not think you are. I am ready to share your perils but I will not lead you against the soldiers.

From A.R. Schoyen: *The Chartist Challenge* (1958)

### Q Harney the Chartist Becomes Harney the Socialist

The earth with all its natural productions [are] the property of all; we denounce all infractions of this natural law as robbery. We believe that the present state of society which permits idlers and schemers to monopolise the fruits of the earth and the productions of industry to be unjust. The principle of universal brotherhood commands that labour and rewards should be equal.

From *Northern Star*, 26 September 1846

### R Harney the International Socialist

It is in the interest of land-lords and money-lords to keep the nations divided; but it is in the interest of the Proletarians, everywhere to unite. And they will unite. From the loom, the anvil and the plow, from the hut, the garret, and the cellar, will come forth, are even *now* coming forth, the apostles of fraternity and destined saviours of humanity.

From *Northern Star*, 11 December 1847

### S Bronterre, in 1836, on the French Revolution

Society has been constituted upon no fixed principles. The state in which we find it is the result of blind chance, the right of the strongest appears to be still the fundamental charter of all 'civilised' states. What the savage does by personal prowess, the civilised man does by cunningly conceived institutions. In trying to escape the evils of savage life, man has unconsciously plunged into another state of false civilisation. To correct the evils of this state was the grand problem to be resolved by the French Revolution.

From Alfred Plummer: *Bronterre* (1971)

### T Bronterre's Solution to the 'Grand Problem'

The end I have in view is social equality for all, to obtain this we must first have political equality for all. To obtain political equality, we must have a more extensive and effective organisation of the working classes, and of that portion of the middle class which is immediately dependent on their custom, than has hitherto been even thought of, much less accomplished.

From *National Reformer*, 7 January 1837

**U O'Brien's Criticisms of the 1832 Reformed Parliament**
What was the first act of that Reformed Parliament? The Coercion Bill
for Ireland. What was the last act of the first session? The New Poor
Law for England. Why did that base Parliament pass both these acts?
To place the labouring classes of both countries at the feet of the
rich assassins, who rob brutalise, and enslave the population of both.

From *McDouall's Chartist Journal*, 31 July 1841

**V His View of the Corrupt House of Commons. Glasgow, 1839**
The present House of Commons represented the fellows who live by
profits, who live by usury; a rascally crew of attornies, bishops and
parsons, pawnbrokers and stockjobbers. It represented men who had
no interest in the welfare of the country. The stockjobber had the
same interest in the public calamity as the pawnbroker had in private
distress. It represented military officers, and about 2,000 brothel-
keepers in London had votes.

From R.G. Gammage: *A History of the Chartist Movement* (1854)

**W His Hope of a Seizure of Power by the People (1839)**
The National Petition is like a bill of exchange and if the House of
Commons dishonours it, Chartists must have recourse to ulterior
proceedings. The Petition can be regarded as a notice to quit, to be
followed up, if necessary by . . . a writ of ejectment. The Convention
has not yet decided whether the ejectment shall be through the door
or out of the window but one thing is certain: an empty house is
better than a bad tenant.

From Alfred Plummer: *Bronterre* (1971)

**X His Rejection of Violence as Self-Defeating (1839)**
Undoubtedly the wild nonsense about *physical force* has done much
mischief. I assert that if the bitterest enemies of the people had sat
down to devise the best means of injuring the people's cause, they
could not have devised more efficient means than by recommending
the people to have recourse to physical force.

From Alfred Plummer: *Bronterre* (1971)

**Y O'Brien Recommends Arming for Self-Defence**
I advise the people to arm to a man to put down by force the traitors
who dare to use force. I call upon you to arm with all possible means.
A large proportion of the Convention is in gaol already. Many of them
have been arrested for riots which the authorities have caused
themselves, as they did in Birmingham.

From *Northern Star*, 3 August 1839

### Z He Regards Technological Developments as Potentially Beneficial

If, instead of working to enrich a few avaricious task-masters at the expense of their slaves, machinery was made to work for the general good by being employed as an auxiliary to, instead of as the antagonist of, human labour, there is no fixing a limit to the blessings that might be derived from it.

From *Poor Man's Guardian*, 13 April 1833

### Aa Public Ownership of National Resources

Railroads should not be private property; neither canals, docks, fisheries, mines, gas, water. Works designed for the use of the public, should be constructed at the public cost and the public should have the advantage. They should not be suffered to fall into the hands of private speculators, for whom they are only a legal disguise to enable them to rob the public.

From Alfred Plummer: *Bronterre* (1971)

### Bb O'Brien's Distaste for the NCA

I could not take part in projects which would imply secrecy, and which would lead to detached movements, to be easily crushed and followed by prosecution. I could not approve of any other than a national movement conducted openly in the broad face of day, under the safeguard of the constitution in which physical force should have no part whatever, unless it began with the oppressor, in which case, the oppressed would be bound to resort to physical force in self-defence.

From *Southern Star*, 26 January 1840

### Cc He Objects to the NCA's Claim to Monopolise the Charter

To bully the entire Chartist body into any one Association, is not the way to promote union. It is a way to promote disunion. To tell a man he is no Chartist, because he does not choose to take out a card will neither convince him that he is no Chartist, nor make him take out a card.

From *The British Statesman*, 5 November 1842

### Dd His Split with O'Connor over the CSU

As no sane person would think of uniting for any purpose with known enemies, our proper business as Chartists, is to combine together as one man, not *with* the middle class, but *against* them, in order to put an end to their usurpations . . .

If they be really friendly, they will unite with us to get *the Charter* – if they be not, they will exclude themselves. We cannot reject any man, of any class, who admits our principles. The People's Charter excludes no one from the rights of citizenship; neither will the Chartists exclude anyone who does not exclude the Charter. But we can form no alliance with men who require that we renounce the Charter.

From *Northern Star*, 24 April 1841

### Ee O'Brien Defends Right to Private Property
Every man has a right to the value of his own produce or services. If one man can do twice the work of another man, he ought to have twice the reward. But if his superior strength or skill gives him the means of acquiring more wealth than his neighbour, it by no means follows that he ought to acquire a right over his neighbour's produce. And here lies the grand evil of society – not in private property, but in the unjust and atrocious powers with which the existing laws invest it. The effects of wealth result not from property, but from robbery – they are not rights of property, but wrongs on industry – they spring from bad laws – from depraved institutions.

From *The English Chartist Circular*, May 1841

### Ff O'Brien's Definition of Class
By the term 'Proletarians' is to be understood persons of both sexes, who were obliged to procure their subsistence by labour, by mendicity, by theft, or by prostitution. Every description of persons who are dependent upon others for the means of earning their daily bread.

From O'Brien: *The Rise, Progress and Phases of Human Slavery* (1849–50)

### Gg His Concern about Chartist Fragmentation, 1849
I will not embroil myself with sectarians (including Chartists). I will discuss only these questions with them, *viz*:
1.  What are the rights the people are entitled to demand?
2.  Would these rights secure for us a real prosperity?
3.  What are the means to enforce these rights?

From Alfred Plummer: *Bronterre* (1971)

### Hh The Aims of the National Reform League
1.  A repeal of our present system of poor laws . . .
3.  The Public Debt, and all private indebtedness affected by the fall of prices should be equitably adjusted in favour of the debtor and productive classes . . .
5.  A sound system of National Credit, through which any man might be enable to rent and cultivate land on his own account.

6. That the Currency . . . be based . . . on real wealth . . . and not the variable and uncertain amount of scarce metal.
7. The State to institute public marts for exchangeable goods, to be valued upon a corn or labour standard.

Principles of the NRL from *The Northern Star*, 30 March 1850

# Questions

**1** Using Sources A-F analyse the ideological differences between Lovett and O'Connor. **(7 marks)**

**2** Examine the views of O'Connor, Harney and O'Brien on the role of violence in Chartist agitation, drawing on the evidence in Sources G-J, N-P, X and Y. **(9 marks)**

**3** From your own knowledge, and Sources B, I, J, L and Bb–Dd, offer an explanation for O'Connor's being either loved or hated within the Chartist movement. **(9 marks)**

**4** 'O'Brien was the theorist of the movement.' What evidence is contained in Sources S-Z to support this view? **(7 marks)**

**5** What light do Sources Q, R, Aa, Ee, Ff and Hh throw upon the socialist ideas of Harney and O'Brien? **(8 marks)**

# 5 CHARTIST MEMBERS

Rank and file Chartist members present an identification problem. Counted in millions, they were mostly anonymous, although some were notable in their locality and played a leading role there. Such leading members often gave anecdotal evidence about the membership at local level, but it often conflicted with that given by the grass roots membership itself [A-D].

A means of reconciling these contradictory impressions is a quantitative approach. David Goodway has analysed London Chartist organisation and suggests that far from being apathetic, it was vigorous during the petition years of 1839, 1842 and 1848 [Table 5.1]. He has further analysed the petition years by month and the peaks of activity seem to occur around the months of greatest Chartist activity in each year [Table 5.2]. These figures relate to London Chartism only. Work on the provincial membership indicates that during 1841 the NCA grew from 80 associations to almost 300 with a total membership of more than 20,000 individuals; by mid–1842 some 400 associations had been set up, with a total membership of over 50,000. Significantly, using the proportion of the local population who were members as a criterion, these associations seem to be stronger in the manufacturing communities than they are in the great urban centres [Table 5.3].

These figures should be treated with caution for they represent only organised Chartism and exclude large numbers of Chartists who were not members of the NCA. They do, however, indicate that many of the assumptions about the type of people who supported the Charter are considerably less than safe. Friedrich Engels, the co-author with Karl Marx of the *Communist Manifesto*, assumed that Chartism was a proletarian movement embracing the industrial working class only, yet Chartism had adherents in the countryside also and Map 5.1 indicates that the movement was widely organised in the west country. This is confirmed by Robert Lowery's description of the people he met when he toured Cornwall in 1839 [E-H].

A further assumption made by earlier historians was that Chartism was a self-contained movement with very little connection with other working-class movements, particularly the trade organisations. Certainly O'Connor advised circumspection to Chartists approaching trade unions, although clearly his advice was not always taken at local level [I & J]. Tables 5.4 and 5.5, which analyse Chartist participation among the trades in both Lancashire and London, suggest a quite different picture; indicating a wide diversity of trade involvement in those regions.

A large number of Chartists were not organised formally. These appeared at the huge mass meetings [3.B], where the size of the crowds is notoriously difficult to estimate with accuracy, although the 'character' of the crowd was often caught by observers. Many people would have been drawn to such an event by the spectacle of the demonstrations. Lowery described such an event on his Cornwall tour where the inclement weather would surely have enticed few casual attenders. Reports of the size of crowds differ widely; estimates of the size of the Kennington Common demonstration of 1848 varied between newspapers and in different editions, or even on different pages, of the same newspaper. The papers studied in Table 5.6 were less than sympathetic to the demonstrators and it could be said that it was in their interests to understate the size of the crowd. But the radical weeklies, published at the weekend after the mass meeting and likely to be more sympathetic towards the petition, indicate the same trend of the unreliability of crowd estimates in the press [Table 5.7].

Perhaps all that can be said with confidence of the number of people who supported Chartism, is that it was indisputably a mass movement. In total, millions of people attended the 'simultaneous meetings', called to consider the ulterior measures in 1839. How many millions is more difficult to assess but the number of genuine signatures upon each of the petitions suggests something between two and three millions. Over the 20 years from 1838 to 1858, it is clear that membership was very fluid. People moved in and out of the movement as active participants, although perhaps they retained their commitment to the Charter. The rank and file of the movement present one of the most frustrating problems to the historian of Chartism, for in addition to their anonymity they continue to be only roughly estimable in number.

## A A Chartist on Lawrence Pitkethly of Huddersfield

Lawrence Pitkethly was for many years a woollen draper in Huddersfield. After a cold ride over Stanedge from Manchester, the first place I used to make for was Pitkethly's and there in his room over the shop he was sure to be met with, surrounded by the most thorough Radicals. I remember with pleasure the old kindly faces and the many warm discussions held by the parties assembled. There was no man better known in the West Riding than 'Old Pitt'.

From *Newcastle Weekly Chronicle*, 19 July 1879

## B Peter Bussey of Bradford was Landlord of the Roebuck Inn, where he encouraged the reading of Chartist Literature

Exceedingly corpulent and in height about five feet nine. His countenance is indicative of thoughtfulness, and of stern resolve. His manners are somewhat rough and his address blunt, though by no means offensive. As a member of the Convention he is exemplary in the discharge of his duties. Without ostentation he is one of the most effective delegates in that assembly.

From *The Charter*, 5 May 1839

### C Local Leaders Often Refer to the Membership. W.G. Burns, a Delegate to the 1839 Convention

The want of sympathy displayed by the working men of London was owing to the high wages which made them contented with their own condition, for, as long as they could procure beef and porter, and enjoy their comforts, they appeared wholly to disregard the miseries and privations of their brethren in the provinces.

From *The Operative*, 31 March 1839

### D Burns Seems at Odds with this London Carpenter

That the workman does not receive a price for his labour that will enable him to procure the necessities of life and that the employer receives more than an equitable profit is evident. Look at the condition of the 'large employer', the major part have risen from the ranks of the journeymen, have accumulated large fortunes, and are the worst enemies of the men. Why?, that a few men may amass largely, while the mass of the trade are reduced to a state of slavery. Then the 'small masters', partly victims of the 'large masters', yet still the victims of avarice and aping to follow the large employers; vieing with them in crushing labour.

From *The Charter*, 14 April 1839

### Table 5.1: Number of London Chartist localities 1838–49

| Year | '38 | '39* | '40 | '41 | '42* | '43 | '44 | '45 | '46 | '47 | '48* | '49 |
|---|---|---|---|---|---|---|---|---|---|---|---|---|
| Number | 13 | 51 | 18 | 39 | 63 | 43 | 27 | 17 | 14 | 23 | 57 | 21 |

* denotes Petition Years.

From David Goodway: *London Chartism 1838–1848* (1982)

### Table 5.2: Number of London Chartist Localities by Month '39, '42 & '48

| Year | Jan | Feb | Mar | Apr | May | Jun | Jul | Aug | Sep | Oct | Nov | Dec |
|---|---|---|---|---|---|---|---|---|---|---|---|---|
| '39 | 20 | 19 | 24 | 38 | 31 | 26 | 24 | 21 | 21 | 22 | 17 | 15 |
| '42 | 31 | 35 | 40 | 42 | 40 | 39 | 39 | 37 | 35 | 38 | 40 | 40 |
| '48 | 21 | 21 | 22 | 26 | 41 | 41 | 36 | 34 | 22 | 22 | 20 | 17 |

From David Goodway: *London Chartism 1838–1848* (1982)

### Table 5.3:  NCA Members in selected Urban and Manufacturing Centres

| Urban Centres* | | | Manufacturing Centres** | | |
| --- | --- | --- | --- | --- | --- |
| | Population | NCA Members | | Population | NCA Members |
| London | 1.873m. | 8,000 | Merthyr | 34,977 | 1,100 |
| Liverpool | 286,000 | 800 | Newport (Mon.) | 13,766 | 400 |
| Manchester | 242,983 | 2,800 | Bilston | 20,181 | 1,000 |
| Birmingham | 183,000 | 1,000–1,200 | Oldham | 42,595 | 700–900 |
| Bristol | 124,000 | 920 | Halifax | 28,000 | 450 |
| Sheffield | 111,090 | 2,000 | Northampton | 21,000 | 600 |
| Newcastle | 70,000 | 1,000 | Loughborough | 10,170 | 800 |
| Bradford | 67,000 | 1,500–1,900 | Trowbridge | 11,050 | 500 |
| Nottingham | 53,091 | 1,650 | Aberdare | 6,471 | 440 |
| Leicester | 53,000 | 3,100 | Keighley | 13,413 | 200 |

\* Large cities (Pop. +50,000) with various industries.
\*\* Smaller towns (Pop. −50,000) with a stronger community sense than the urban centres, one industry predominant.

From Dorothy Thompson: *The Chartists* (1984)

### E Engels Sees Chartists as Proletarians

It is natural that they should put a proletarian law in place of the legal fabric of the bourgeoisie. This proposed law is the People's Charter, which is purely political and demands a democratic House of Commons. In the unions opposition has always remained isolated: single working men or sections have fought a single bourgeois. But in Chartism it is the whole working class which rises against the bourgeoisie, and attacks the political power with which the bourgeoisie has surrounded itself.

From F. Engels: *The Condition of the Working Class in England* (1844)

### F Rural Chartism

Very many, in the country districts, walk, on a Saturday night, after a week's toil, as many as three, four, five, or six miles to the country town, fearful of taking the *Star* from the village agent, under the nose of the village tyrant.

From *Northern Star*, 9 January 1841

### G Elliot Yorke, MP for Cambridge, Describes his Constituency

If gentlemen think there is nothing to be dreaded from our rural labourers, I fear they are greatly mistaken. I do not believe there is any village in my neighbourhood that would not be ready to assert by *brute force* their right (as they say) to eat fully the fruit arising from their own labour.

From *Cambridge Chronicle*, 28 March 1846

### H Robert Lowery on Cornish Workers

The working-classes were a simple primitive people, with strong religious feelings quick in their perceptions of subjects which came within their experience. But they knew little of general society, its state or conflicting opinions. Living in a remote corner of the land, they had not mixed with the rest of the population. Here as elsewhere in England we found the average mind and manners of the women much superior to the men among the more uneducated poor. Their powers of thinking had evidently been more exercised.

From Robert Lowery: *Passages in the Life of a Temperance Lecturer* (1856–57)

### I O'Connor's Advice to Chartists Seeking Trade Union Co-operation

Attend their meetings, swell their numbers, and give sympathy, but on no account interpose the Charter as an obstacle. All labour must unite; and they will discover that the Charter is the only standard under which they can successfully rally.

From *Northern Star*, 16 November 1844

### Table 5.4: Trades attending the Kersal Moor Meeting 1838

| Textile Trades | Metal Trades |
|---|---|
| Cotton-Spinners | National Associated Smiths |
| Dressers and Dyers | Smiths and Wheelrights |
| Calenders | Smiths and Farriers |
| Fustian Cutters | Mechanics |
| | |
| Building Trades | Clothing Trades |
| Stonemasons | Men's shoemakers |
| Marble masons | Ladies' shoemakers |
| Carpenters and Joiners | Tailors |
| Painters and Plasterers | |
| Bricklayers | |
| Labourers (of Bricklayers?) | |

From Robert Sykes: 'Early Chartism and Trade Unionism in South-East Lancashire', in Epstein and Thompson: *The Chartist Experience* (1982)

## Map 5.1: Branches of the NCA in 1841

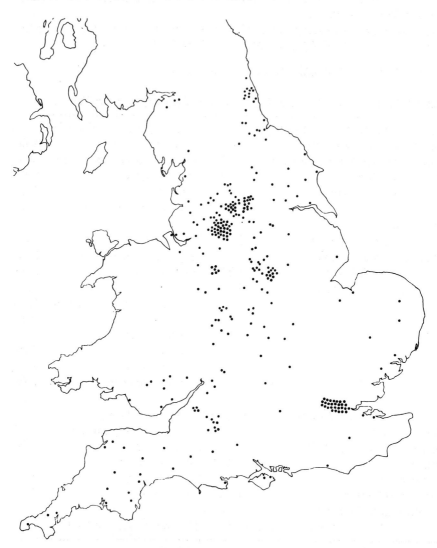

From David Jones: *Chartism and the Chartists* (1975)

### J Bolton Chartists Show no such Reservations in 1839: Address to the Bolton Trade Societies from the Bolton WMA (1839)

There are numbers of your members who have joined our ranks in the struggle for freedom, and we have scarcely an enemy amongst you. Yet your Delegation of Adhesion in Bodies, – as has been done at Birmingham, Newcastle, Manchester, Oldham and Bury and other places – to the great principles we advocate, is absolutely necessary, the adoption of which can alone rid you of the tyrannical interference of your Oppressors . . .

We request meetings of your different Trades electing Delegates to confer with the WORKING MEN'S ASSOCIATION.

From Dorothy Thompson: *The Early Chartists* (1971)

### Table 5.5: Index of Chartist Participation Among London Trades

| +4.00 ('outstandingly Chartist') | | +2.00 ('markedly Chartist') | |
|---|---|---|---|
| Newsagents/Newsmen | 10.58 | Silk-weavers | 3.66 |
| Newspaper editors/Reporters | 9.27 | Gold and Silver workers | 3.56 |
| Printing trades | 6.40 | Bookbinders | 3.41 |
| Coffee-house keepers | 6.18 | Printers | 3.33 |
| Hatters | 6.16 | Fellmongers/leather | |
| Stonemasons | 5.44 | dyers | 3.26 |
| Boot and Shoemakers | 5.38 | Chair makers | 2.58 |
| Coppersmiths/brazier | 5.30 | Carpenters and Joiners | 2.48 |
| Carvers and Gilders | 4.52 | Tin-plate workers | 2.47 |
| Carvers and Gilders | 4.52 | Tailors | 2.4 |
| | | Curriers/leather dressers | 2.38 |
| | | Plasterers | 2.30 |
| | | Engineers and | |
| | | millwrights | 2.29 |
| | | Typefounders | 2.21 |
| | | Cabinet makers | 2.08 |

| +1.00 ('having a propensity to Chartism') | | | |
|---|---|---|---|
| Metal trades | 1.91 | Other building trades | 1.30 |
| Jewellers, gold and silver | | Bricklayers | 1.26 |
| smiths | 1.53 | Gardners and | |
| Upholsterers | 1.51 | Nurserymen | 1.12 |
| Clock and Watchmakers | 1.41 | Boilermakers | 1.10 |
| Painters and Glaziers | 1.40 | | |

(14 Trades with an Index of −1.00 have been omitted.)

From David Goodway: *London Chartism 1838–1848* (1982)

### K Meeting on Skircoat Moor, Halifax, August 1842

At two o'clock in the afternoon, a meeting of from ten to fifteen thousand people was held. After the business of the meeting, the greater part of the multitude remained encamped on the moor. A great number of them stretched themselves on the heather, in large circular groups, having a great many women amongst them, singing Chartist hymns and songs . . .

The snatches of conversation which might be heard amongst these groups seemed to be of firm determination. The women were extremely excited, and we heard several of them urging the men to rescue the prisoners who had been taken in the morning; one exclaimed 'If I wor a man, they sudn't be long there'; another said 'Ye're soft if ye don't fetch 'em out to neet'. These women, who appeared from their dialect, to be chiefly Lancashire women were not without their effect, and appeared to be gathering spirit and determination to make the attempt.

From *The Halifax Guardian*, 20 August 1842

### L Robert Lowery's Cornish Tour 1839
We had arranged a final meeting at Gwenapp Pit. Although the day was very unfavourable, upwards of 14,000 people were assembled, and stood to hear us for upwards of two hours in the rain.

From Robert Lowery: *Passages in the Life of a Temperance Lecturer* (1856)

### Table 5.6: Estimates of Crowd at Kennington Common (1848)

| Newspaper | Estimated Crowd Size | |
|---|---|---|
| | April 10th. Edition. | April 11th. Edition. |
| Evening Sun | 150,000 | – |
| Evening Express | 100,000 | 15,000 |
| London Telegraph | 80,000–100,000 | – |
| Shipping & Mercantile Gazette | 100,000 | 50,000 |
| Evening Standard | 9,000–10,000 | 10,000 |
| The Times | 20,000 | (Editorial) 10,000–20,000 (Report) 20,000–50,000 |

From David Goodway: *London Chartism 1838–1848*, (1982)

### Table 5.7: Press Estimates of Crowd Size on Kennington Common 1848

| Newspaper | Estimated Crowd Size |
|---|---|
| Northern Star | 250,000 |
| Lloyd's Weekly | (Report) 100,000 (Editorial) 2–300,000 |
| Weekly Dispatch | 50,000–200,000 |
| The Nonconformist | 150,000 |

From David Goodway: *London Chartism 1838–1848*, (1982)

# Questions

1 With reference to Sources A-D examine the problems which the study of the rank and file membership presents to the historian. **(7 marks)**

2 What trends are indicated by Tables 5.1–5.3, and what are the strengths and limitations of this type of data? **(8 marks)**

3 Assess the value to the historian of Sources E-H and Map 5.1. **(7 marks)**

4 Using Sources I and J and Tables 5.4 and 5.5, discuss the assertion that trade unionists remained aloof from Chartism. **(9 marks)**

5 What conclusions may be drawn about the size of Chartist membership from Sources K and L and Tables 5.6 and 5.7? **(9 marks)**

# 6 CHARTIST WOMEN

Nineteenth-century chroniclers of Chartism, such as R.G. Gammage, were anxious to portray the movement as responsible and feared that any emphasis upon the contribution of women may trivialise it. Because of this, historians have paid scant attention to women Chartists. Recent work has shown that they played a far more significant role than had been believed previously. Female radicalism among the working classes was not regarded as in any way extraordinary before the Chartist years, although by the 1840s journalists seem anxious to discredit the movement and frequently described the women within it as crude, vulgar and vaguely disreputable [A-C].

Male Chartists do not seem to have been averse to female suffrage. Writing in Lancaster prison in 1840, R.J. Richardson composed a pamphlet which he called *The Rights of Woman*, echoing Thomas Paine's *Rights of Man*. Richardson argued in favour of the right of women to vote, founding his argument upon the important contribution made by women to the economy, although in so doing he reveals much to us of the male attitude towards women and their role in early Victorian society [A-F].

By the late 1830s changes in industrial organisation had forced an increasing number of women and children to seek employment outside of the home in the new factories and mills. There they were subjected to a discipline which women resented because it restricted their traditional roles of wife and mother. Little female criticism can be found of the patriarchal family in which women were subject to male authority. On the contrary, they seemed willingly to accept a role which was supportive rather than independent of their menfolk. Women expressed more immediate grievances, the press-gang and the New Poor Law of 1834 being foremost. They were preoccupied with the practical difficulties which beset family life. Many working-class women's organisations were set up during the late 1830s and early 1840s. Such a group in East London discouraged the discussion of controversial subjects such as the law on marriage or religion. This group stressed the more pressing problems of poverty, or the relief for families of political prisoners and recommended 'exclusive dealing' [3.K]. They seem to perceive their Chartist role as auxiliary to the male campaign [F&G].

Richardson expressed outrage at the effects of industrial change upon women. He harboured a romantic ideal of womanhood, which was common in his day. This stereotype is illustrated by his use of such cliches as 'the fairest and tenderest of God's creatures' or 'our fair friends'. In his analysis of the economic role of women he digressed to describe their brutalisation through heavy manual labour on the land, in the coal mines and in the textile mills. Finally, he returned to a stout defence of women's rights. He was not alone in his view, both Lovett and Collins argued at length on the subject of sexual equality as part of their proposed educational programme to raise the standards of the workers to a level of respectability that would render them acceptable within the political system [H-N].

Their emphasis was placed upon the educational function of the maternal role. Lovett appeared to hold a view similar to Robert Owen [8.E], who believed that 'individual and social character is overwhelmingly determined by the environment'. Lovett regarded the mother as an indispensable ingredient in the environment, and through her influence to 'improve' the working classes [O-S].

Women Chartists seemed to have changed their style of political action in the mid-1840s. There developed a tendency towards a more restrained, if not constrained, pattern of public behaviour for women. This may have filtered down socially from middle-class public conduct. Only the most forceful of individual women were able to resist the pressures which drove them into 'respectability', and they were subjected to considerable public ridicule and abuse [T-V].

## A The Woman Chartist's Role

They seldom spoke on public platforms, these women presented banners, made and presented gifts to visiting speakers and invariably marched in the great processions usually at the head.

From Dorothy Thompson: *The Chartists* (1984)

## B The Women of Skircoat Green Mourn the 'Peterloo' Dead in 1819

The women of this village were not behind the men in their love for liberty, for I have heard my mother tell of their having regular meetings and lectures at the house of Thomas Washington, a shoemaker; she well remembered the name of Mr Camm; and they, too, went into mourning and marched in procession, Tommy's wife carrying the cap of liberty on the top of a pole. I was not surprised at the people being so earnest in the cause of Reform when I heard my mother tell how the people had to suffer; when she was a girl she brayed sand for a neighbour, getting some potato parings for it, which her mother boiled and they ate them.

From Benjamin Wilson, 'The Struggles of an Old Chartist' 1887. In David Vincent: *Testaments of Radicalism* (1977)

### C Chartist Meeting on Clerkenwell Green, London, June 1848

There was a sprinkling, too, of women among the crowd, their shrill voices, and not very choice phraseology, indicating their presence, when the intervening mob prevented their being seen.

From *The Times*, 1 June 1848

### D Male Chartists Were not Averse to Female Suffrage

I may say here that the first draft of the Bill, afterwards called the People's Charter, made provision for the suffrage of women, but as several members [of the LWMA] thought its adoption in the Bill might retard the suffrage of men it was unfortunately left out.

From William Lovett: *My Life and Struggles* (1876)

### E Richardson on Female Suffrage

Ought women to interfere in the affairs of state?

If a woman is qualified to be a queen over a great nation, armed with power of nullifying the powers of Parliament, by parity of reason, a woman in a minor degree ought to have a voice in the election of the legislative authorities.

From R.J. Richardson: *The Rights of Woman* (1840)

### F On Women's Contribution to the Economy

Women contribute to the wealth and resources of the kingdom. The dairy is managed almost exclusively by women: the small livestock wholly so. See the number of females who are employed in milking and making butter and bringing them to market.

There are fewer females employed in [mining] because of the greater strength of body and mind required to undergo the fatigue and danger; one third of those employed in mining are women, more especially in the coal mines.

We come now to the manufacturing population. Here then is a population principally employed in manufacturing cotton to the extent of £200,000,000 annually and principally females too.

From R.J. Richardson: *The Rights of Woman* (1840)

### G The Manifesto of the Newcastle-upon-Tyne Female Political Union

FELLOW-COUNTRYWOMEN, – We call upon you to join us and help our fathers, husbands, and brothers, to free themselves and us from political, physical, and mental bondage . . .

We have been told that the province of woman is her home, and that the field of politics should be left to men; this we deny. Is it not true that the interests of our fathers, husbands, and brothers, ought to be ours? If they are oppressed and impoverished do we not share those evils with them? If so, ought we not to resent the infliction of those wrongs upon them? We have read the records of the past and our hearts have responded to those women, who struggled against tyranny and urged their countrymen to be free or die.

Because the husband's earnings could not support his family, the wife has been compelled to leave her home neglected and, with her infant children, work at a soul and body degrading toil.

For years we have struggled to maintain our homes as our hearts told us should greet our husbands after their fatiguing labours. Even now our husbands are overwrought, our houses half-furnished, our families ill-fed, and our children uneducated.

We have seen the father dragged from his home by a ruffian press-gang, compelled to fight against those that never injured him, paid only 34/- [£1.70p.] per month, while he ought to have had £6; his wife and children left to starve or subsist on the scanty fare doled out by hired charity. We have seen the poor robbed of their inheritance and a law enacted to treat poverty as a crime, to deny misery consolation, to take from the unfortunate their freedom, to drive the poor from their homes and their fatherland, to separate those whom God has joined together, and tear the children from their parents' care.

From *Northern Star*, 2 February 1839

### H East London Female Patriotic Association
Objects:
1st.  To unite with our sisters in the country, and to assist our brethren in obtaining Universal suffrage.
2nd.  To aid each other in cases of great necessity or affliction.
3rd.  To assist any of our friends imprisoned for political offences.
4th.  To deal as much as possible with those shopkeepers who are favourable to the People's Charter.
Laws and Qualification of Members:
6th.  That no gentleman be admitted without invitation of a majority of the members present.
8th.  That no person shall be allowed to lecture on religious subjects or on the marriage laws, except by the invitation of all the members present.

From *The Charter*, 27 October 1839

### I Richardson on the Condition of Women in Agriculture
In the fields we find women performing every kind of labour except, draining, fencing, ploughing and mowing. In the barn, with the exception of thrashing and handicraft work, women perform every other occupation. Inure to such toils and hardships, she becomes masculine; and the force of all those tender passions implanted by

God in the breast of woman to temper the ruggedness of man, become weakened, her real virtues forgotten, and her proper usefulness destroyed. To the women I say throw off the degradation of predial slavery*, return to your domestic circles and cultivate your finer feelings for the benefit of your offspring. How can you expect to be free, when you nourish a new race of hereditary bondsmen?

* 'Predial slavery'; bondage relating to work on land.

From R.J. Richardson: *The Rights of Woman* (1840)

### J Women in the Coal Mines
It is no uncommon thing to see them suspended by a rope in the act of being lowered several hundred feet below the surface of the earth into the mine, where *they draw waggons laden with coal* to the bottom of the shaft ready to be raised up, and also where they squat down on their knees, hewing with a small pick the coal from the seam. To see them at meal times rising from the mouth of the shaft, more 'like demons from the deep' than those angelic creatures, our poets call women, is a sight that would 'harrow up the souls of men', if they possessed the feelings of humanity, and create a feeling of disgust that can allow 'woman, lovely woman', to be forced by poverty from her domestic duties down these hell holes of coal mines.

From R.J. Richardson: *The Rights of Woman* (1840)

### K In the Textile Mills and the Ideal Female Social Role
Many years before the age of puberty, they are taken to these *hell-holes* to earn their little pittance. Oppressed by fatigue, fed with insufficient diet, their little minds abused, their bodies scourged, their frames wasted, the pith of womanhood dried up and withered, they grow up deformed in body, or die prematurely with the first attack of disease; some are women and mothers before their natural period. The wife will rise from her marriage bed at five o'clock in the morning and with her husband proceed to the mill, there is no honeymoon for them. Should she be 'as ladies wish to be as love their lords', there is no ease, no time for nourishment and rest for her:- work, work, work, until the latest moment of her travail; there must be no time wasted no steam wasted, toil she must, until nature, bursting through the tyrant's laws, forces her to relinquish her life of slavery to give birth to her burden.

From R.J. Richardson: *The Rights of Woman* (1840)

### L Richardson Returns to Women's Rights
Woman bears her share of the burdens of state and contributes more than her fair proportion to the wealth of the country. I ask you, is there

a man, knowing these things, who can lay his hand upon his heart and say, Woman ought not to interfere in political affairs? No: I hope there is none for the honour of my sex.

From R.J. Richardson: *The Rights of Woman* (1840)

### M Lovett and Collins on the Family
Intellectual men would regard their *homes* and *families* with far different sensations than are felt by those who seek for pleasure and gratification anywhere rather than at home. Rightly constituted minds would feel that, of all other pleasures, *those that spring from domestic happiness are the most enduring and substantial*. Esteeming their wives as *their equal companions*, and not as the mere slaves of their passions, they would labour to cultivate their [wives'] mental powers and be the better prepared to train up their children in knowledge, virtue, and the love of freedom.

In the plan of the NATIONAL ASSOCIATION, we have provided for the admission of *female* members on the same conditions as *males*.

From William Lovett and John Collins: *Chartism* (1840)

### N They Argue for Sexual Equality
As regards politics, *the law does not exempt women from punishment any more than men*; therefore, by all *just* constitutional arrangements, *all should share in the enactment of laws to which they are amenable*. If a woman be a *householder*, she must contribute her share of *direct taxes*; and if not, on all her eating, drinking, and wearing, she contributes her share of *indirect taxes* equally with men: and according to the unperverted spirit of our constitution, *there should be no taxation without representation*. Again, if a woman is married, *her influence* is still exercised in all the political affairs of her husband; and if *single*, her political knowledge or ignorant prejudices are equally powerful. Therefore, their rights and influence being manifest, the necessity for their *political instruction* must be equally obvious.

From William Lovett and John Collins: *Chartism* (1840)

### O Their Concept of Motherhood
Women are *the chief instructors of our children*, whose *virtues* or *vices* will depend more on the education given them by their mothers than any teacher. If a mother is deficient in knowledge and depraved in morals, her prejudices, habits, and conduct will make the most lasting impression on her children. If she is so well informed as to fix in her children habits of cleanliness, order, refinement of conduct, and purity of morals, the results will be evident in her wise and well-

regulated household. But if, in addition, she be richly stored with intellectual and moral treasures, and makes it her chief delight to impart them to her offspring, they will, by their lives and conduct, reflect her intelligence and virtues throughout society.

From William Lovett and John Collins: *Chartism* (1840)

### P James Watson Remembers His Mother's Influence

I had but one parent to do the duty of two, and I am proud to say that duty was performed with all a mother's kindness and devotion. My mother, although poor, was intelligent, as a proof of which I may state that she was a teacher in one of the Sunday-schools in the town. To my mother I owe my taste for reading and what school education I received. I could read well, write indifferently, and had a very imperfect knowledge of arithmetic. I remembered my mother reading *Cobbett's Register*, and saying she wondered people spoke so much against it; she saw nothing bad in it, but a great many good things.

From William J. Linton: *James Watson. A Memoir* (1880)

### Q Mothers As Educators

Our first ideas are received from a mother's eye, and much of our temper and disposition depend on the characters we trace there. As our perceptions are awakened and faculties matured, her wise or foolish conduct towards us leaves lasting impressions of good or evil. Seeing that so much of our early education depends on the mental and moral qualities of women, should we not labour to qualify them for these important duties? And when we take into account *how much of men's happiness depends upon the minds and dispositions of women* how many cares their prudence can prevent, and their sympathy and kindness can alleviate, it ought to redouble our anxiety to promote the education and *the social and political rights of women*.

From William Lovett and John Collins: *Chartism* (1840)

### R This Chartist's Father Receives the Maternal Attention

Father was a drunkard, a great spendthrift, an awful reprobate. The late Mr. Isaacs used to lecture on Tuesday evenings and she was constantly begging my father to go and hear him, without avail; she would always get ridiculed for her pains till he offered himself to go if mother would treat him to some gin. She did, and we all three went; father scoffing and swearing, and mother inwardly praying on our journey. Presently I noticed the altered looks of father, and as the minister seemed to increase in energy father literally trembled so that several of the congregation noticed it. At length the service ended, and directly we got out, father said, 'Mary my dear, let us go home. God have mercy upon me, a miserable sinner.' From that time till he died he was a changed man . . .

The consequences of this remarkable change in my father did not better our circumstances. Mother and I became outdoor paupers.

From John James Bezer, 'The Autobiography of One of the Chartist Rebels of 1848' (1851). In David Vincent: *Testaments of Radicalism* (1977)

### S She is too Busy Surviving to Attend to his Education

My education was very meagre; I learnt more in Newgate than at my Sunday School. I ought to have learned a great deal in fifteen years. Yet, what had I learned? to read well, and that was all. I knew nothing of arithmetic, and could scarcely write my own name.

From John James Bezer, 'The Autobiography of One of the Chartist Rebels of 1848' (1851). In David Vincent: *Testaments of Radicalism* (1977)

### T The Changing Image of Female Conduct

Their presence in the early years of the movement cannot be questioned. In the opposition to the Poor Law, in the early demonstrations, processions and social organisations of all kinds they played a central part. Somewhere around the mid-forties, however, the nature of their participation changes. The number of women in the Chartist crowd seem to diminish, the rough confrontational action which occurred in the early years disappears.

Perhaps the women were gaining a changed perception of themselves and of their social role. Such activities as smoking and drinking, indulged in when funds permitted in the early industrial communities, became increasingly frowned upon as relaxations for women. The growth of temperance, the increasing attempt to reclaim the working population for organised Christianity, and the spread of 'provided' education for both sexes, all helped to impose a less rough, more domestic, more genteel image of female behaviour.

The change in the tactics of the authorities in handling crowds may also have kept some women away from meetings and demonstrations. The decade of the 1840s saw the introduction of police forces in many areas under the provisions of the Rural Police Act of 1839. It could be that mass demonstrations began to assume a generally rougher nature. The photograph of the crowd on Kennington Common in 1848 seems to suggest that very few women were present.

From Dorothy Thompson: *The Chartists* (1984)

### U Ernest Jones and 'Respectability'

Do you suppose the thoughtful and self-respecting, or the respecter of democracy, will go, and by his presence help to drag it down and desecrate it in the pot-house? We want the support and countenance of woman in our movement – for the Charter must become a domestic spirit, a tutelar saint, a household god, before it can arise a legislative power! And what shall make it so, – but the support of woman? That which does not emanate from a million homes, will have no lasting basis even amid the cheering of a thousand platforms. It is woman that ever sways the mind of man – it is woman that ever moulds the character of the child. And would you take your wives, sisters, and daughters, to the pothouse, among the reek of gin and porter, the fume of foetid pipes, and the loose ribaldry of incipient intemperance?

From Ernest Jones: 'Raise Chartism from the Pothouse.' *Notes to the People* (1852)

### V A *Punch* Caricature of Woman Chartist, Mary Anne Walker

# Questions

**1** What insights are given into the participation of women in the
Chartist movement by Sources A-C, T and U? **(7 marks)**

**2** Study Sources D-F, L and N and summarise the Chartist arguments
for female suffrage. Explain why it was not included in the Six Points.
**(7 marks)**

**3** To what extent are the problems which concerned women illustrated
by Sources G, H and V? **(8 marks)**

**4** How valuable to the historian are Sources I-K as evidence about the
everyday life of working-class women in the 1830s and 1840s?
**(8 marks)**

**5** Using your own knowledge and Sources O-S examine the female role
in early Victorian society. **(10 marks)**

# 7 CHARTISTS AND THE LAND

The Chartist attempt to provide land for the deprived was not a new idea. The seventeenth-century radical Gerrard Winstanley had argued for the right of all to possess land and the idea was developed by Thomas Paine and others during the pre-Chartist years. During the late eighteenth and early nineteenth centuries vast numbers of people were driven from the land by enclosure and industrialisation. Therefore, many Chartists were at most only one generation removed from rural life. The stark reality of industrial society encouraged a nostalgic yearning to return to the countryside. Adam Rushton expressed this sentiment [A-C].

Influenced by his direct experience of the landlord system in Ireland, Feargus O'Connor had long held strong views on the question of individual land ownership. In 1843 he published a pamphlet outlining his land plan and the benefits it would bestow upon resettled industrial workers. Later in the same year a Chartist conference in Birmingham approved the plan in principle, but two further years elapsed before the Chartist Land Society was established. Progress continued slowly and it was early 1847 before the society was reorganised into the Chartist Land Co-operative Company [D-F].

The scheme was bitterly opposed. Some believed it was unworkable, some thought it was illegal. Thomas Cooper broke with O'Connor over this issue, and O'Brien attacked the scheme because it seemed to be inconsistent with O'Connor's position on the 'New Move' [3.L-O]. O'Brien also opposed the plan on ideological grounds; he believed that no-one should own land; that it was the property of all and should be managed by the state. This was part of O'Brien's vision of a new society, socialist in character, which the Charter would create. The land, a major means of producing wealth, should not be privately owned for individual profit, but available for all to use for the benefit of society as a whole. O'Connor disagreed. He believed in private land ownership and frequently explained his opposition to O'Brien's collectivism in the Land Company's journal. The differences between the two Irishmen were irreconcilable and even while O'Connor's scheme flourished, O'Brien pressed on with his own proposal and when he founded the NRL [4.Hh] he made state control of all land a basic plank in its platform [G-N].

Despite intense opposition, the scheme had its successes. In March 1846 land was acquired at Heronsgate near Watford and the first 'O'Connorville' was inaugurated to be formally opened amid much publicity and celebration in May 1847. Stimulated by this success, the Land Company had organised about 240 branches throughout the nation by mid-1847 [Map 7.1]. Some 250 people were resettled by the company on its five 'O'Connorvilles' before the organisation fell foul of the law, as did so many Chartist endeavours [8.]. Public criticism of the scheme from outside the Chartist ranks led to a House of Commons Select Committee hearing on its legality. O'Connor stoutly defended his scheme before the committee and explained the purpose behind it. When the committee reported in August 1848, it became clear that the company was deemed to be illegal and would have to be wound up. Eileen Yeo describes this as just one of the problems which Chartists constantly faced in law. Ernest Jones, who became leader of the Chartists after 1848, had initially supported the land plan as a means of breaking the hold of employers over their employees through the absorption of surplus labour, but after the company's collapse he modified his view, calling for government use of waste land as a way of alleviating poverty [O-V].

The land scheme failed to achieve its primary aim of resettling industrial workers in sufficient numbers to change society. The reasons for that failure are debatable, but the derision heaped upon O'Connor has distorted the history of the Chartist movement, particularly in relation to his land plan. That the scheme was poorly organised and badly managed is not in question. Indeed, its failure proved too much for O'Connor, who after ten exhausting years of work for the movement, began to break down mentally under the strain. However, his land plan was not a total failure. It had served as a rallying point for the Chartists during the years 1843–48 when the Charter itself appeared increasingly unattainable, and its supporters needed something more practical to rally around. Some Chartists felt that perhaps it was a scheme before its time [W & X].

## A The New Law of Righteousnesse, (January 1649)
All the men and women in *England*, are all children of this land, and the earth is the Lord's, not particular men's that claims a proper interest in it above others . . .

Was the earth made for to preserve a few covetous, proud men, to live at ease, and for them to bag and barn up the treasures of the earth from others, that they might beg or starve in a fruitful Land, or was it made to preserve all her children?

From G.H. Sabine: *The works of Gerrard Winstanley* (1941)

## B Thomas Spence on the Land
The land was claimed by a few, and divided among themselves, in as assured manner as if they had manufactured it. They fell into a

habit of acting as if the earth was made for or by them, and did not scruple to call it their own. Thus men may not live in any part of this world, not even where they are born, but as strangers, and by the permission of the pretender to the property thereof.

From Thomas Spence: *The Real Rights of Man* (1793)

### C A Chartist Veteran's Thoughts on Land

What interested me most at these [Chartist] meetings was the question of the Land, which was earnestly discussed. My father had always the earth hunger upon him, and so had I. Should I ever be able to possess a few acres of freehold to make an earthly paradise? This was a question I pondered over frequently and long.

From Adam Rushton: *My Life as Farmer's Boy, Factory Lad, Teacher and Preacher* (1909)

### D O'Connor on the Right to Land

The land belonged to the people; those who by their capital and labour cultivate it. The labourers ought to possess the earth. But as for soldiers, police, judges, barristers, bishops, and parsons, they swarmed, in this unhappy country, like locusts, devouring every green thing, and making that which should be paradise hell on earth.

From *Northern Star*, 13 July 1839

### E On the Benefits of Access to Land

It is his pride to rise rejoicing in the reflection that upon his industry the whole family must depend; while, in return, he looks for that contentment which a happy home can alone bestow. If he should be overworked he dreads not the awful sound of the factory bell. He is not deprived of the comfort of the society of his wife; he is not degraded by living as a prostitute upon her and his children's labour. He is not reduced to the humiliating necessity of shaking his slumbering babe into a kind of artificial life, in order that she may obey the capitalist's morning summons. He is master of himself and of his time.

From Feargus O'Connor: *A Practical Work on the Management of Small Farms* (1843)

### F Rules and Regulations of the Chartist Land Co-operative Company Objects of the Society

To purchase land on which to locate such members as may be selected, to demonstrate to the working classes of the kingdom — firstly, the value of land, as a means of making them independent of grinding capitalists; and, secondly to shew them the necessity of securing the speedy enactment of the 'People's Charter', which should do for them nationally, what this society proposes to do sectionally: the accomplishment of the political and social emancipation of the enslaved and degraded working classes.

### Membership

All persons are eligible to become members by taking out a card of membership, and a copy of these rules, for which the sum of fifteen pence [6p.] shall be paid; one shilling [5p.] to be an instalment of the share.

### Means

£5,000 raised in shares at £2 10s. [£2.50] each would purchase 120 acres and locate sixty persons with two acres each, leaving a balance which would be sufficient to build a commodious and comfortable cottage on each allotment.

### Selection of Occupants

The selection of occupants for the allotments to be by lot from amongst those who may have paid up their shares.

From *Northern Star*, 3 May 1845

## G Thomas Cooper Opposes O'Connor's Land Scheme

Occasionally, I called upon O'Connor, and he invariably expounded his Land Scheme to me, and wished me to become one of its advocates. But I told him I could not; and I begged him to give the scheme up, for I felt sure it would bring ruin and disappointment upon himself and all who entered into it. All he said in explication of his scheme only served to render it wilder and worse in my estimation . . .

The growth of O'Connor's Land Scheme rendered him haughty towards me, when he found he could not reckon on me as one of his helpers. I forbear to enter into the recital of the fierce quarrel I had with O'Connor about his land scheme.

From Thomas Cooper: *The Life of Thomas Cooper* (1872)

## H O'Brien Points to O'Connor's Inconsistency

The strangest thing of all that Feargus should have dragged millions of people to torch-light meetings, demonstrations etc., all attended with great sacrifice of time and money, and caused the ruin of thousands through imprisonment, loss of employment and expatriation, when all the while he had only to establish a 'National Chartist Co-operative Land Society' to ensure social happiness for us all, and when he had discerned that 'political equality can only spring from social happiness'. Formerly he taught us that social happiness was to proceed from political equality; but doubtless when his land-bubble has burst, he will have the old or some other new creed for us.

From *National Reformer*, 15 May 1847

### I O'Brien's View of the Land
Labour betters the land, but does not create it. Why then does a band of villains dare to say, 'the land is ours'? The land has three values:
1. The original value of land;
2. The improvements in land;
3. The capabilities of land for yielding value.

The first and third belong forever to the nation. The second may be claimed by the improver.

From *True Scotsman*, 6 July 1839

### J O'Brien Proposes State Management of Land
An enlightened government, representing all classes, would [not] allow commerce to be conducted as it is now. Such government would place commerce and manufactures upon a totally different footing, and make the land the common property of all, without any real or material injury to the existing proprietors.

From *The English Chartist Circular*, May 1841

### K O'Connor Advocates Private Land Ownership
I am advocating the co-operative system, not the principle of communism. My plan is entirely opposed to communism, for I repudiate communism and socialism. My plan is based upon the principle of individuality of possession and co-operation of labour.

From F.C. Mather: *Chartism and Society* (1980)

### L O'Connor Attacks Socialism
Communism either destroys wholesome emulation and competition, or else it fixes too high a price upon distinction and must eventually end in the worst description of despotism – the despotism of self-surrender and non-reliance on self; whilst upon the other hand individual possession and co-operation of labour creates a wholesome bond between all classes of society, which none can push beyond the will or requirement of his neighbour.

From *The Labourer*, I, 149, 1847

### M O'Brien Describes Private Land Ownership as a Social Evil
What a chain of evils follows upon the usurpation of the soil! What a rapid striking off of the links of the chain would follow upon the

nationalisation of landed property! Only prevent one set of men from making God's 'gift to all' their private property, and that moment you open the door to unlimited improvement.

From *National Reformer*, 17 April 1847

### N The Principles of O'Brien's National Reform League
2. To appropriate the present surplus revenue to the purchasing of lands and the location thereon of the unemployed poor.
4. The gradual resumption by the State (on the acknowledged principles of equitable compensation to existing holders, or their heirs) of its ancient, undoubted, inalienable dominion and sole proprietorship over all the lands, mines, turbaries, fisheries etc, of the United Kingdom and our colonies; to be held by the State as trustee, in perpetuity, for the entire people, and rented out to them in such quantities, and on such terms as the law and local circumstances shall determine.

From *Northern Star*, 30 March 1850

### O The Inauguration of Heronsgate (March 1846)
He [O'Connor] stood there rejoicing in being the best abused man, not in England, but in the world. He was called a leveller, but he laughed the name to scorn; he was an elevator. He required new land marks for a new population as he required new books for new minds. Fences nine yards wide, occupying over six acres of this farm, were the old land marks; a post and a rail would be the new land marks. (Cheers.) An old farmhouse built of lath and plaster, and tiles, was the old land mark; the labourer's cottage built of brick, of the best brick, stuccoed outside, and with gutters, were the new land mark. (Loud cheers.)

From *Northern Star*, 22 August 1846

### P Feargus Opens the First O'Connorville (May 1847)
What I now witness is but a feeble outline – a meagre unfinished sketch of that full-length portrait of freedom, happiness and contentment which will eventually result from the novelty I have ventured to propound. (Cheers.) While joy fills your hearts here, the song of gladness resounds throughout the land. (Cheers.)

From *Northern Star*, 8 May 1847

### Q Ernest Jones Commemorates the Occasion with a Poem
In crowded town where poor mechanic wakes.
But why today, at twilight's earliest prime,
When moon's grey finger points the march of time,

Why starts he upwards with a joyous strength
To face the long day slavery's cheerless length?
Has freedom whispered in his wistful ear,
'Courage poor slave! deliverance is near?'
Oh! she has breathed a summons sweeter still:
'Come! take your guerdon* at O'Connorville!'

\* guerdon – reward.

From *Northern Star*, 22 August 1846

## Map 7.1: Branches of the National Land Company (Summer 1847)

From David Jones: *Chartism and the Chartists* (1975)

**R O'Connor Mocks his Audiences to Publicise his Land Plan**
You are, in a word, a poor, beggarly, lousy set of devils! Without house or home, or bread, or clothes, or fuel; begging the means of subsistence, and thankful to him who will coin your sweat into gold! . . .

Now mark what you might be! Just what you have made others, comfortable, independent, and happy! thanking no man for the means of subsistence!

From Donald Read and Eric Glasgow: *Feargus O'Connor, Irishman and Chartist* (1961)

**S O'Connor before the Select Committee (1848)**
I had always thought that it was a strong inducement to a man to work out his own salvation without parochial relief, to work as many hours as he chose, and go to his own bed when he desired instead of going to the workhouse. I think that a man working and having regard for himself, every day in the year, will be much more likely to cultivate resources of the country to the highest state of perfection than a man working for another at so much remuneration. I was determined to establish a settlement where the poor man could estimate the value of his own labour, below which he would not sell it in the market.

From F.C. Mather: *Chartism and Society* (1980)

**T Chartism's Problems with the Law**
The Chartist search, over ten long years, for an adequate and legal form of national organisation reveals what a potent shaping and ultimately deforming influence the State was, whether it was showing an iron fist, as custodian of public order suppressing Chartist militancy, or wearing a velvet glove, as framer of legislation giving legitimacy and protection to selected forms of working-class association. The land scheme collapsed, exhausted by its attempts to clear the hurdles of the law and debilitated by internal difficulties.

From Eileen Yeo, 'Some Practices, and Problems of Chartist Democracy'. In Epstein & Thompson (Eds): *The Chartist Experience* (1982)

**U Jones Criticises the Monopoly in Land (1847)**
Wages must be kept constantly falling. And how do they effect the fall? By *surplus labour*. How do they obtain the surplus labour? By monopoly of the land, which drives more hands than are wanted into the factory. By monopoly of machinery, which drives those hands into the street. Then planting their foot upon that living base of surplus, they press its aching heart beneath their heel, and cry

'Starvation! Who'll work? A half a loaf is better than no bread at all', and the writhing mass grasps at their terms.

From *New York Tribune*, 25 August 1852

### V Jones Modifies His View (1850)

There is nothing more reactionary than the small freehold system. It is increasing the strength of landlordism. Let the Government divide the waste lands among the people – they would support the entire pauper population, and thus relieve the artificial labour market. Instead of building workhouses, erect Colleges of Agriculture: instead of emigration promote home colonisation.

From J. Saville: *Ernest Jones, Chartist* (1952)

### W The Failure Encourages Further Press Criticism

Every estimate seemed to be made on the supposition of a perpetual miraculous interposition. Every acre was to yield on an *average* such crops as no acre ever did yield except under the rarest combinations of favouring climate, consummate skill, and unlimited manure – and then only occasionally. Every cow was to live for ever, and was to give more milk than any save the most exceptional kine ever gave before, and was never to be dry. Every pig was to be a prize one – every goose to be a swan.

From *Edinburgh Review*, Vol. XLV, (1852)

### X Chartists Remain Unconvinced that O'Connor Is to Blame

O'Connor tried to grapple with the land question. A great many thousands became members, several of my friends cheerfully made great sacrifices to raise the money. Feargus had a great many difficulties to contend against, for he had nearly all the press in the country against him, whilst a great many got on the land who had no knowledge of it, and what with the opposition outside and the dissatisfaction within, the company was thrown into Chancery. Two or three from Halifax went on the land, but the scheme was before its time; yet I believe the day is not far distant when it will be successfully carried out.

From Benjamin Wilson: *The Struggles of an Old Chartist* (1887). In David Vincent (Ed.): *Testaments of Radicalism* (1977)

## Questions

1 Using Source F, and your own knowledge, explain why the Chartist Land Plan was implemented. **(4 marks)**

**2** In what ways do Sources J and S differ in their views as to how the land might be used to improve the condition of the working class?

**(7 marks)**

**3** With reference to Source V, indicate some of the social problems which prevailed during the Chartist period. **(7 marks)**

**4** Consider the value to the historian of Sources J, V, and S as evidence of disunity among the Chartists. **(8 marks)**

**5** Describe the later history of the Land Plan and consider its contribution to the Chartist movement. **(9 marks)**

# 8 CHARTISTS AND PUBLIC ORDER

Chartism was born of illegality. It developed out of the Reform Act agitation, the unstamped press campaign, and the anti-Poor Law protest. Radicals in the 1830s could barely act without breaking the law, and there were many instances when working-class radicals fell foul of it. The case of the Tolpuddle martyrs in 1834, and that of the Glasgow Cotton Spinners in 1837, ended in transportation for some and imprisonment for many others. The tactics the early radicals used tended to be passive resistance to unjust law, in which they knowingly broke the law and were prepared to suffer the consequences for doing so. This was a highly effective form of protest for it highlighted the repressive nature of the law, and mass defiance was an important weapon in the radical armoury [A-C].

The Chartists were acutely aware of the dangerously narrow path which they trod between legality and illegality and, despite their efforts to remain legal, the challenge which pre-Chartist radicals presented to the law and the violent language used by the early Chartists, created a profound fear of revolution among the propertied classes. Torchlight processions symbolised popular anger and frightened them into thinking that they would be the victims of incendiarism (the burning of property). A Royal Proclamation on New Year's Day 1839 declared such processions to be illegal, although they continued to be held in some places. In the same year a Rural Police Act was passed which created an outcry among the working class and became a major Chartist grievance [2.W]. Many so-called 'physical force' Chartists were merely defending what they believed was the constitutional right of the people to arm themselves in self-defence. After the risings of 1839 and 1840, over 500 Chartists were arrested and imprisoned. Among them was Bronterre O'Brien, who was almost jubilant in his response to the repressive policy of the government. It is paradoxical that the judge at his Newcastle trial accepted the right of the people to possess arms, but declared it illegal to use them [D-G].

In 1842, when the 'Plug Plot' strikers were rampant in the Potteries and the North of England, troops were moved from London to control the disorder. They were an indispensable part of the apparatus for maintaining public order and were far from popular among the people. The experiences of Thomas Cooper both in the courts and in Stafford Gaol for his part in the 'Plug Plot' are typical of those endured by many Chartists, whom it seems were regarded as political prisoners.

Cooper clearly was by no means an ideal prisoner and he took every opportunity to harass the authorities [H-L].

The effectiveness of government repression during the early 1840s eased the minds of the propertied classes, but their fears were re-enlivened in 1848 when revolution in France stimulated Chartist interest in a third petition. John Saville argues that by then the forces of law and order were very well developed. Some Chartists claimed that police presence at demonstrations provoked more violence than it prevented. As the Kennington Common demonstration of April 1848 drew near, the authorities prepared to control any disorder which might follow their ban upon the proposed march across the bridges towards parliament. After the demonstration had dispersed and the petition ridiculed, a number of outbreaks of disorder and rioting took place throughout the country. By then the government had refined their intelligence gathering techniques through spies and informers, and were able to control these attempts at insurrection [M-Q].

There seemed to be a note of resignation in O'Connor's speech to the 1848 convention when he tried to explain both the government's ban of the march upon parliament and his acquiescence in it. Perhaps he recognised what seems evident to historians today: that by 1848 the mass demonstration, with its banners, bands and marching columns, was no longer a viable form of political action for the working class. The power of the state had become too great; it could now impose its own conditions upon demonstrations and rallies, thereby rendering them less potent, even less awesome than that of 1831 when Robert Lowery's huge crowd at Newcastle almost dared the authorities to enforce the law against them [R].

## A Robert Lowery Describes an Illegal Rally (1831)

The excitement on the Reform Bill now agitated all classes of the community; it developed thought among the more reflecting, and begat discussion on the principles of government and national prosperity. It produced thinkers indeed in every class and more especially the working classes. Out of this thinking the after movements of the working classes originated, and from this arose some of their errors also. Frequently a hundred thousand people would come to meetings which were held on Newcastle Town Moor, the surrounding villagers marching in rank with military step, to bands of music. It is well known that the language was often violent, and the opposition was threatened with physical resistance if they should proceed to enforce any laws to stop the unions in agitating their demands.

From Robert Lowery: *Radical and Chartist* (1856–1857)

## B The 'Unstamped' Press Campaign

In 1831 I became a member of the National Union of the Working Classes. The price of the newspaper stamp was fourpence for each newspaper. The object of Mr. Hetherington and others, was to get that tax abolished. To effect this, the *Poor Man's Guardian*, and other papers circulating amongst the working classes, introduced *news* into their columns. To suppress the sale of these publications was the aim of the government. After sending 600 persons to prison, they were compelled to reduce the price of the stamp from fourpence to one penny, its present price. To get rid of this penny is the object of the 'Society for the Abolition of the Taxes on Knowledge'. . .

In this year Mr. Hetherington suffered his first six months' imprisonment in Clerkenwell prison for publishing the *Poor Man's Guardian*.

The cholera being very bad all over the country, the government ordered a 'general fast'. The National Union, to mark their contempt for such an order, determined to have a procession through the streets of London and afterwards have a general feast. In April I was arrested with Messrs Lovett and Benbow, for advising and leading the procession. We were liberated on bail, tried and all acquitted. Towards the end of this year Mr. Hetherington was sentenced to his second six months confinement . . .

In February, 1833, I was summoned at Bow Street for selling the *Poor Man's Guardian*. I justified my conduct before the magistrates in selling unstamped newspapers. They considered me as bad as my friend Hetherington, and sentenced me to six months in Clerkenwell prison.

From James Watson: 'Reminiscences of James Watson'. In David Vincent (Ed.): *Testaments of Radicalism* (1977)

## C J.R. Stephens Condemns the New Poor Law

If this damnable law, which violated all the laws of God, was continued, and all means of peaceably putting an end to it had been made in vain, then, in the words of their banner, 'For children and wife we'll war to the knife'. If the people who produce all wealth could not be allowed to have the kindly fruits of the earth which they had raised by the sweat of their brow, then war to the knife with their enemies, who were enemies of God. If the musket and the pistol, the sword and the pike were of no avail, let the women take the scissors, the child the pin or needle. If all failed, then the firebrand – aye the firebrand – the firebrand I repeat. The palace shall be in flames. If the cottage is not permitted to be the abode of man and wife, and if the smiling infant is to be dragged from a father's arms and a mother's bosom, it is because these hell-hounds of commissioners have set up the command of their master the devil, against our God.

From *Northern Star*, 10 November 1838

### D R.J. Richardson Tries to Avoid Illegal Measures
He did not advise them to make a run upon [the] banks, to make any alarm in the country; but he advised them to look sharply after what they had in [the] savings' banks. To advise a run on these banks was illegal; to advise them to embarrass the Government in money matters was illegal; but to advise them to look after their own was perfectly legal, and just, and reasonable. He would say to them, do not go to the savings banks, because it might chance that they would get their money, and the people of Manchester would get none; but let us know when you are ready and we would all go together. Only give us a fair start. If the Government had not the people's hard cash to trust to, the army would be disbanded, and the navy laid up in dock. He did not advise them to take that help from the Government, but he did not think that they should be so foolish as to lend a man a stick, and ask them to thrash them.

From R.G. Gammage: *A History of the Chartist Movement* (1854)

### E Sir H.E. Bunbury to the Home Secretary, 24 December 1838
I must confess that the present state of the Kingdom gives me much uneasiness. I am fully sensible of the vast power inherent in the classes possessing property; nor does it seem probable that any insurrection of the working classes would succeed ultimately in establishing a democratical government on the ruins of the Constitution. But I do fear that a wide-spreading insurrection of the working people is far from improbable, and that it may be attended with so much destruction of property, and such a shock to trade & credit & confidence as would be ruinous to this Commonwealth . . .

The present time is very fit & favourable for reforming our militia system, and I have been glad to hear that you have a plan in preparation. I hope that it will be connected with the organisation of an effective Police for the rural districts.

From F.C. Mather: *Chartism and Society* (1980)

### F O'Brien's Response to Government Repression
It has come at last! The Government of law has all but ended in England; the Government of the Sword has already begun. In one more brief month every gaol in England will be crammed. In one month more there will not survive a vestige of liberty in the land, except for those usurpers and murderers of society who call you 'mob' and style themselves as the 'higher and middle Orders'. . .

The object of the rich is to drive you unarmed, unorganised and unprepared into rebellion, in order that they may cut down the bravest of you in small sections, strike terror into the rest, and bring up your leaders, and thus crush the movement altogether.

From *Northern Star*, 10 August 1839

### G The Judge Sums up at O'Brien's Newcastle Trial (1840)

The language he admits using is very strong, even intemperate, but he cannot be punished for that. The real question is whether it was calculated to produce the effects charged in the indictment. The procuring of fire-arms is not an unlawful act, the people have a right to have arms; but the question is whether they were to get these arms for the purpose of using them against the public peace. But I must here remark what a dangerous thing it is to incite the people to arm, and to make them the sole judges of whether they had a right to interfere.

From Alfred Plummer: *Bronterre* (1971).

### H Facsimile of a letter from J. Mansfield of Leicester to M. Heathcoat of Hinkley, 19 August 1842, reporting an armed Chartist meeting

**I The Grenadier Guards Are Harassed by a London Mob**
They were followed by a large crowd of persons, which continued
during their progress to increase by accumulations of women and
boys, until their arrival at the railway station. Murmurs of groans, and
hisses burst from the crowd, which continued to increase as they
advanced up Regent-street, mingled with exclamations of 'remember
you are brothers'. About the middle of Regent Street, the crowd
pressing so closely on the band, the officer in command directed the
band to strike playing, and at the same time ordered the soldiers to
'fix bayonets'. That, however, did not silence the groans and hisses,
which were uttered by the crowd until the battalion reached the
terminus.

From *The Observer*, 14 August 1842

**J Troops Fire upon Preston Strikers**
The mob then proceeded down Lune-street, followed by the military,
and when near the Corn-exchange halted. The Riot Act was then read,
and Chief-constable Woodford, and Mr. Banister, superintendent of
police, endeavoured to persuade the mob to retire, for fear of
consequences; and while so engaged, one of the rioters aimed a
stone so surely at Captain Woodford that it felled him to the ground,
and while there he had the brutality to kick him. Immense bodies of
stone were now thrown at the police and soldiers, many of the former
being much hurt, and part of the mob having gone up Fox-street they
then had the advantage of stoning the military from both sides. Under
these circumstances, orders were given to fire; the military
immediately obeyed, and several of the mob fell. This did not appear
to have much effect, for one fellow came out in front of the mob and
when in the act of lifting his hand to throw a stone, was singled out
by one of the 72d. who fired, and he fell. This appeared to put a
damper on the proceedings of the mob, and they began to separate.
It is scarcely known how many have been wounded, but it is supposed
12 to 15, some of them mortally.

From *The Times*, 15 August 1842

**K Thomas Cooper Describes Conditions in Stafford Gaol (1843)**
Each cell had a stone floor; was simply long enough to hold a bed,
and broad enough for one to walk by the side of it. An immense slab
of cast iron formed the bedstead, and it rested on two large stones.
A bag stuffed so hard with straw that you could scarcely make an
impression on it with your heel formed the bed. Two blankets and a
rug completed the furniture. There was no pillow; I had a very large
and heavy travelling cloak. If I had not brought this with me, I could

not have slept in that cell during the winter without becoming a cripple, or losing my life.

The prison-bell rang at half-past-five, and we were expected to rise and be ready to descend into the day-yard at six. At eight they brought us a brown porringer, full of 'skilly' – unpalatable oatmeal gruel – and a loaf of coarse, dark-coloured bread. At noon, they unlocked the door of our day-room, and threw upon the table a netful of boiled potatoes, in their skins, and a paper of salt for dinner. At five in the evening, they brought us half a porringer of 'skilly'; but no bread. At six we were trooped off, and locked up in our sleeping cells for the next twelve hours.

From Thomas Cooper: *The Life of Thomas Cooper* (1872)

### L He is Evidently a Political Prisoner
You shall be allowed to write to your wife and receive letters from her; but all letters must be delivered *open* by yourself to the governor, and he will open all letters from your wife, before he delivers them to you. In the course of time we may allow you, also, to correspond with two or three friends, – so long as they are not political . . .

You have no objection to our seeing the books, I hope? If they be political, we should object to your having them.

From Thomas Cooper: *The Life of Thomas Cooper* (1872)

### M The Efficiency of Public Order Agencies
From the 1790s the coercive powers of the state had been tested and slowly improved in confrontation with a succession of radical and democratic movements; and by the 1840s, the last decade of mass demonstrations, there was now a much more efficient administrative apparatus than ever before. 1848 showed a notable improvement in security matters than the earlier years of the forties, mainly because of the large-scale mobilisation of special constables.

From John Saville: *1848* (1987)

### N A Working Man, (M.H. Molyneux), Protests at Police Violence. Anti-Tax Riot in Trafalgar Square (March 1848)
The conduct of your officers Was quite Sufficient to create instead of quelling a disturbance for example at 10 Past 4 o'clock, Policeman 105F Threatened to Knock some Respectable men ass over Head, for no offence, at 4 o'clock Policeman 131F Said (by way of Bravado) there is plenty of us left to Kill 4 or 500 more. at 23 minutes past 4. 147D was amusing himself By Pushing a Boy off the Steps of St. Martin's Church at 25 minutes to 5 at least 30 of your officers made

a rush towards the Strand and took a man Prisoner. Surely
Gentlemen there was enough officers to take 1 Prisoner without
Splitting his head open.

From David Goodway: *London Chartism 1838–1848* (1982)

## O The Authorities Make Ready for Disorder (April 1848)

A breastwork of sandbags, with loopholes for muskets and small guns
had been thrown up along the parapet wall of [the Bank of England],
at each corner of the building, musket batteries, bullet proof, were
raised, having loopholes for small carronades.

The line of the road from the Strand to the new Houses of
Parliament has all the appearance of a thoroughfare in a besieged
capital. Notices from the Police Commissioners, that no carts, vans
or omnibuses are to be allowed upon the road from Abingdon-street
to Cockspur-street after eleven o'clock, and that no delay is to be
permitted in the other streets, agitate the public, and the appearance
of patrols of mounted police, and of single files of soldiers in the
usually quiet street, is ominous and alarming.

From *Northern Star*, 15 April 1848

## P Violence in Yorkshire after the Petition's Rejection

A great meeting of Chartists of the West Riding was held on Good-
Friday on Skircoat Moor, being one of a series held throughout the
country in conformity with a recent recommendation of the National
Chartist Convention held in London. It was the largest meeting held
in Yorkshire during the year [1848]. A large meeting was also held on
Toftshaw Moor, near Bradford, at which physical force was strongly
advocated and the people recommended to arm themselves. Matters
now began to look serious. There had already been riots in Bradford
and other parts. The authorities in Bradford became greatly alarmed,
and issued a proclamation that processions with banners and bands
of music would not be allowed to enter the town, but when the
meeting was over they folded up their banners and thousands of
them marched in procession towards Bradford; on our arrival on the
outskirts of the town we were met by a large number of special
constables, accompanied by horse and foot soldiers. I was standing
with two Halifax friends in a cross street when they came up; they
arrested the men who had the banner poles and made them prisoners.
The horse soldiers were ordered to clear the mob, and they dashed
up the street with drawn swords slashing in all directions, causing us
to run as fast as we could, they galloping after us; we climbed over
a high wall into some gardens just in time to get out of their way.
When we got back into the street we found it almost empty. One

man to whom we had been talking (who was neither a Chartist or attended the meeting) received a sword wound in the shoulder.

From Benjamin Wilson: *The Struggles of an Old Chartist* (1887)

### Q Police Infiltration of Chartist Meetings (January 1840)

A meeting of Chartists took place last Saturday night, at which it was first agreed to commence insurrectionary acts on the following (Sunday) morning, but in consequence of a discovery having been made that spies were present at the meeting, the original intentions were abandoned, and the meeting was adjourned to Tuesday evening, when it was resolved, on account of the opposition of some influential members to defer for the present any overt act of riot or insurrection. There is to be a meeting of the Chartists tonight (Thursday) at which if not disturbed by the presence of what they call spies a final resolve will be come to.

From David Goodway: *London Chartism 1838–1839* (1982)

### R Feargus Explains to the Convention

Now he would wish the Convention to put themselves into the place of the Government, and say whether if they heard that an armed demonstration was to take place, they would not have felt it their duty to meet it, and endeavour to prevent the peace being destroyed? – Had it not been for the folly of some persons out of the Convention – and a few in it – there would never have been any opposition to their demonstration.

From *Northern Star*, 15 April 1848.

# Questions

**1** 'To be a working-class radical in the 1830s, was to confront the Law.' What illustration of this statement can be found in Sources A-D?

**(7 marks)**

**2** How far do Sources E-G explain the authorities' response to Chartist agitation? **(7 marks)**

**3** Using Sources I, J, and N-Q, examine the means used to contain the 'Chartist threat'. **(8 marks)**

**4** What is the value of Sources K and L to the historian studying the attitudes and experiences of Chartist prisoners? **(9 marks)**

**5** To what extent is the assertion in Source M confirmed by Sources Q and R? **(9 marks)**

# 9 THE ECONOMIC BACKGROUND TO CHARTISM

The foundations of economic thinking in the Chartist years had been laid in 1776, with the publication of Adam Smith's *Wealth of Nations*. He had asserted that individual self-interest and minimal government regulation were basic to a sound economy. This theory of *laissez-faire* influenced the later thinkers of the nineteenth century. The economic background to Chartism was one of change. The population, which had begun to grow around 1500, exploded after 1800 [Table 9.1]. This population growth preoccupied the political economists of the day, among whom was Thomas Malthus. Around 1800 he wrote copiously upon the subject, arguing that increased population created surplus labour, and thus unemployment and poverty. The problem of poverty, he argued, was therefore insoluble because it was subject to natural laws. This theory became labelled Malthusianism, and led radicals to detest him; Cobbet referred to him as 'the Beastly Malthus' [A & B].

As Malthus had suggested, population growth was unsustainable without a proportionate increase in wealth produced. Patrick Colquhoun observed how this extra wealth had been created in what amounted to a transformation of the British economy; from being predominantly agricultural, Britain became the major manufacturing nation in the world [C., Tables 9.2–9.5].

One of the effects of this expansion in the creation of wealth was a new perception of the economic function of labour. It came to be regarded as a commodity to be bought and sold at market prices which were regulated by the size of the population. This disturbed many observers, notably Robert Owen, sometimes dubbed 'the Father of British Socialism', who endeavoured to ameliorate the effects of this economic change upon the working classes [D, E. & Table 9.6].

Another effect was the stimulus which increased production gave to Britain's foreign trade. It was intensified by such developments as the railways and steam-powered shipping. This gave rise to the development of the idea of 'Free Trade', advocated by devotees of Adam Smith, who regarded any limitations upon trade in the form of import duties to be economically harmful. They found the Corn Laws to be particularly damaging. These laws had been introduced in 1815 after the French wars, to regulate the importation of cheap foreign corn and protect domestic grain from competition. To the Free Trade school, they appeared to inhibit the export of manufactured goods and thus the free market abroad. They were also criticised because they seemed to maintain artificially high food prices to the benefit of the landed interest but to the detriment of the labouring classes. In 1838 the ACLL was founded to campaign for repeal. Although its contribution to repeal in 1846 is a matter of disagreement among historians, the League undoubtedly focused attention upon the issue. Richard Cobden and John Bright spearheaded the campaign, which eventually advocated free trade generally [F. & Tables 9.7, 9.8].

Economic growth was not a continuous upward movement. It was punctuated by periods of stagnation or slower growth known as troughs, followed by periods of further or swifter growth ending in peaks. Such a cyclical pattern of economic activity suggests that prosperity was not universally or continuously experienced by those in the manufacturing classes. Since the 1920s the impact of this economic change upon the lives of the working classes has been debated among historians in what has become termed the 'Standard of Living' controversy. Sir John Clapham was the first to challenge the traditional view that the condition of the working classes worsened during the period. Other historians took up the argument and were labelled either 'Optimists', (those who thought conditions improved), or 'Pessimists', (those who argued the opposite case). In more recent years attempts have been made to clarify the arguments, although it seems that the debate will always engage the interest of economic historians because of the difficulties of methodology [Table 9.9 & G-L].

## A The Theory of Laissez-faire
Every individual is continually exerting himself to find out the most advantageous employment for whatever capital he can command. It is his own advantage, and not that of society, which he has in view. But the study of his own advantage naturally leads him to prefer employment which is most advantageous to society . . .

By pursuing his own interest he frequently promotes that of society more effectually than when he really intends to promote it. I have never known much good done by those who affected to trade for the public good . . .

To give the monopoly of the home market to the produce of domestic industry is in some measure to direct private people, and must be either a useless or a hurtful regulation. If the produce of domestic can be bought there as cheap as that of foreign industry, the regulation is evidently useless. If it cannot, it must generally be hurtful.

From Adam Smith: *The Wealth of Nations* (1776)

## B Malthus on Population Growth
When the population of a country increases faster than usual the labouring classes must have a greater quantity of food than they had before for the maintenance of their families . . .

The great increase of population in late years has been owing to the power of the labouring classes to obtain a greater quantity of food, partly by temporary high wages in manufactures, partly by the increased use of potatoes, partly by increased task-work and the employment of women and children, partly by increased parish allowances to families, and partly by the increased relative cheapness of manufactures and foreign commodities . . .

What is essentially necessary to a rapid increase in the population is a great and continued demand for labour; and this is proportioned to the rate of increase in the quantity and value of those funds which are actually employed in the maintenance of labour.

That a continued increase of population is a powerful and necessary element of increasing demand, will be most readily allowed; but that the increase of the population alone, or, the pressure of the population hard against the limits of subsistence, does not furnish an effective stimulus to the continued increase of wealth, is confirmed by universal experience. If want alone, or the desire of the labouring classes to possess the necessaries and conveniences of life, were a sufficient stimulus to production, the earth would probably before this period have contained, at the very least, ten times as many inhabitants as are supported on its surface at present.

From Thomas Malthus: *Principles of Political Economy* (1836)

**Table 9.1: Population Growth in Great Britain (in 000s) 1801–1851**

| Year | Total Population | Male | Female |
|------|------------------|--------|--------|
| 1801 | 10,501 | 4,994 | 5,507 |
| 1811 | 11,970 | 5,700 | 6,271 |
| 1821 | 14,092 | 6,833 | 7,259 |
| 1831 | 16,261 | 7,885 | 8,376 |
| 1841 | 18,534 | 9,020 | 9,515 |
| 1851 | 20,548 | 10,156 | 10,677 |

From B.R. Mitchell: *European Historical Statistics 1750–1970* (1975)

**C Patrick Colquhoun Observes the Growth in Manufacturing**
It is impossible to contemplate the progress of manufactures in Great Britain within the last thirty years without wonder and astonishment. Its rapidity exceeds all credibility. The improvement of the steam engines, but above all the facilities afforded to the great branches of the woollen and cotton manufactories by ingenious machinery, invigorated by capital and skill, are beyond all calculation; and as these machines are rendered applicable to silk, linen, hosiery and various other branches, the increased produce, assisted by human

labour, is so extensive that it does more than counterbalance the difference between the price of labour in this, and other countries.

From Patrick Colquhoun: *A Treatise on the Wealth, Power, and Resources of the British Empire* (1815)

### Table 9.2: Index of Industrial Production in Great Britain 1801–1850
(1850=100)

| Year | '01 | '10 | '15 | '20 | '25 | '30 | '35 | '40 | '45 | '50 |
|------|-----|-----|-----|-----|-----|-----|-----|-----|-----|-----|
| Index | 24 | 29 | 32 | 36 | 46 | 54 | 61 | 71 | 86 | 100 |

From B.R. Mitchell: *European Historical Statistics 1750–1970* (1975)

### Table 9.3: Index of Industrial Production in Great Britain 1835–1850
(1850=100)

| Year | '37 | '38 | '39 | '40 | '41 | '42 | '43 | '44 | '45 | '46 | '47 | '48 | '50 |
|------|-----|-----|-----|-----|-----|-----|-----|-----|-----|-----|-----|-----|-----|
| Index | 68 | 68 | 71 | 71 | 75 | 79 | 79 | 82 | 86 | 86 | 89 | 93 | 100 |

From B.R. Mitchell: *European Historical Statistics 1750–1970* (1975)

### Table 9.4: Consumption of Raw Materials (000s tonnes) 1816–50

| Year | Coal | Pig Iron | Raw Cotton |
|------|------|----------|------------|
| 1816 | 16,200 | – | 40 |
| 1818 | – | 330 | 50 |
| 1820 | 17,700 | 374 | 54 |
| 1823 | 19,200 | 462 | 70 |
| 1825 | 22,300 | 591 | 76 |
| 1830 | 22,800 | 688 | 112 |
| 1835 | 28,100 | 1,016 | 144 |
| 1840 | 34,200 | 1,419 | 208 |
| 1845 | 46,600 | 1,537 | 275 |
| 1850 | 50,200 | 2,285 | 267 |

From B.R. Mitchell: *European Historical Statistics 1750–1970* (1975)

### D Ricardo Discusses the Price of Labour

Labour, like all other things which are purchased and sold, and which may be increased or diminished in quantity, has its natural and its market price. The natural price of labour is that price which is necessary to enable the labourers to subsist and perpetuate their race, without either increase or diminution.

It is when the market price of labour exceeds its natural price, that the condition of the labourer is flourishing and happy, that he has it in his power to command a greater proportion of the necessaries and enjoyments of life, and therefore to rear a healthy and numerous family. When however, by the encouragement which higher wages give to the increase of population, the number of labourers is increased, wages again fall to their natural price, and indeed from a re-action sometimes fall below it.

When the market price of labour is below its natural price, the condition of the labourers is most wretched. It is only after their privations have reduced their number, or the demand for labour has increased, that the market price will rise to its natural price.

From David Ricardo: *Principles of Political Economy and Taxation* (1817)

### Table 9.5: Percentage of National Product by Economic Sector 1788–1850

| Year | 1788 | 1801 | 1811 | 1821 | 1831 | 1841 | 1850 |
|---|---|---|---|---|---|---|---|
| Agriculture | 40% | 33% | 36% | 26% | 24% | 22% | 21% |
| Industry and Construction | 21% | 23% | 21% | 32% | 35% | 35% | 35% |
| Transport, Communications and Commerce | 12% | 17% | 17% | 16% | 18% | 19% | 19% |

From B.R. Mitchell: *European Historical Statistics 1750–1970* (1975)

### Table 9.6: Labour Force by Economic Groups (in millions) 1841 & 1851

| Year | 1841 | | 1851 | |
|---|---|---|---|---|
| Gender | Male | Female | Male | Female |
| Agriculture, etc | 1.458m. | .081m. | 1.824m. | .230m. |
| Mining | .218m. | .007m. | .383m. | .011m. |
| Manufacturing | 1.816m. | .639m. | 2.349m. | 1.263m. |
| Construction | .376m. | .001m. | .496m. | .001m. |
| Commerce and Finance | .094m. | .001m. | .091m. | − |
| Transport/Communications | .196m. | .004m | .433m. | 013m. |
| Services | .459m. | 1.041m. | .482m. | 1.241m. |
| Others | .474m. | .041m. | .438m. | .075m. |

From B.R. Mitchell: *European Historical Statistics 1750–1970* (1975)

### E Robert Owen Calls for Care of 'Living Machines'

Since the introduction of inanimate mechanism into manufactories, man has been treated as a secondary and inferior machine; and far more attention has been given to perfect the raw materials of wood and metals than those of body and mind. Give due reflection to the subject, and you will find that man, even as an instrument for the creation of wealth, may be still greatly improved . . .

Adopt the means which ere long shall be rendered obvious to every understanding, and you may not only partially improve those living instruments, but learn how to impart to them such excellence as shall make them surpass those of the present and all former times.

Instead of devoting all your faculties to invent improved inanimate mechanism, let your thoughts be directed to discover how to combine the materials of body and mind, which, by a well devised experiment, will be found capable of progressive improvement . . .

Let us not perpetuate the evils which our present practices inflict on this large proportion of our fellow subjects. A well-directed attention to form the character and increase the comforts of those who are so entirely at your mercy, will essentially add to your gains, prosperity and happiness, no reasons, except those founded on ignorance of your self-interest, can in future prevent you from bestowing your chief care on the living machines which you employ. By so doing you will prevent human misery, of which it is now difficult to form an adequate conception.

From Robert Owen: *A New View of Society* (1813)

### Table 9.7: Volume of British Merchant Shipping 1790–1850

| Year | Number of Ships | | Tonnage |
| | Sail | Steam | (in 000s tons) |
| --- | --- | --- | --- |
| 1790 | 13,557 | | 1,383 |
| 1800 | 15,734 | | 1,699 |
| 1810 | 20,253 | | 2,211 |
| 1814 | 21,449 | 1 | 2,414 |
| 1820 | 21,935 | 34 | 2,439 |
| 1830 | 18,876 | 298 | 2,198 |
| 1835 | 19,797 | 503 | 2,360 |
| 1840 | 21,883 | 771 | 2,768 |
| 1845 | 23,471 | 917 | 3,123 |
| 1850 | 24,797 | 1,187 | 3,565 |

From B.R. Mitchell: *European Historical Statistics 1750–1970* (1975)

## F Richard Cobden Attacks Sir Robert Peel

You said that your object was to find more employment for the increasing population. Who so likely, however, to tell you what markets could be extended as those who are engaged in carrying on the trade and manufactures of the country? [You] must know that all parties in the manufacturing and commercial districts disapprove of [your] laws. The Corn-law is in such a state that no regular merchant will engage in the corn trade. How can [they] send out orders for corn, when there is no certainty whether they shall have to pay the 20s.[£1.00] duty, or any less sum, when it arrives? . . .

Take, again sugar. The right hon. Gentleman reduced the duties on 700 articles, and he carefully omitted those two articles which are supplied by North and South America, the only two countries the trade of which can resuscitate our present declining manufactures. He took the duty off caviare and cassava powder, but he left corn and sugar oppressed with heavy monopoly duties . . .

I admit that the reduction of the duty on timber is a good thing; but you reduced the duty when there are 10,000 houses standing empty within a radius of twenty miles of Manchester, and when there are crowds of ships rotting in our ports. At the same time, you denied our merchants the means of traffic by refusing to reduce the duties on the two most bulky articles which our ships carry.

From Richard Cobden, 'Speech in the House of Commons, February 17th, 1843'. In *Speeches on Questions of Public Policy by Richard Cobden M.P.*: Edited by John Bright and James E. Thorold Rogers (1903)

**Table 9.8: Length of Railway Line (in kilometres) 1825–1850**

| Year | 1825 | 1830 | 1835 | 1840 | 1845 | 1850 |
|------|------|------|------|------|------|------|
| Kms | 43 | 157 | 544 | 2,390 | 3,981 | 9,797 |

From B.R. Mitchell: *European Historical Statistics 1750–1970* (1975)

**Table 9.9: Annual Turning Points of Trade Cycles 1828–54**

| Peak Year | 1828 | 1831 | 1836 | 1839 | 1845 | 1854 |
|-----------|------|------|------|------|------|------|
| Trough Year | | 1829 | 1832 | 1837 | 1842 | 1848 |

From W.W. Rostow: *British Economy of the Nineteenth Century* (1948)

## G Sir John Clapham Challenges the Orthodox View

The legend that everything was getting worse for the working man, down to some unspecified date between the drafting of the People's Charter [1837] and the Great Exhibition [1851], dies hard. The fact that, after the price fall of 1820–21, the purchasing power of wages in general was definitely greater than it had been just before the revolutionary and Napoleonic wars, fits so ill with the tradition that it is very seldom mentioned, the work of statisticians on wages and prices being constantly ignored by historians.

From Sir John Clapham: *The Economic History of Modern Britain* (1926)

### H  T.S. Ashton Represents the 'Optimists'

During the period 1790–1830 factory production increased rapidly. A greater proportion of the people came to benefit from it both as producers and consumers. The growth of trade unions, friendly societies, savings banks, newspapers and pamphlets all give evidence of a large class raised well above the level of mere subsistence.

There were however, masses of unskilled or poorly skilled workers, whose incomes were almost wholly absorbed in paying for the bare necessaries of life, the prices of which remained high. My guess would be that the number of those who were able to share in the benefits of economic progress was larger than the number of those who were shut out from these benefits and that it was steadily growing.

From T.S. Ashton: 'The Standard of Life of Workers in England 1790–1830'. *Journal of Economic History*, Supp. IX, 1949

### I  E.J. Hobsbawm: A 'Pessimist'

It is altogether likely that living standards improved over much of the eighteenth century. It is not improbable that, sometime soon after the onset of the Industrial Revolution [1780s] they ceased to improve and declined. Perhaps the middle 1790s mark the turning point. At the other end, the middle 1840s certainly mark a turning point.

From E.J. Hobsbawm, 'The British Standard of Living, 1790–1850'. *Economic History Review*, Vol X, No. 1, 1957

### J  E.P. Thompson Distinguishes 'Way' from 'Standard' of Life

It is quite possible for statistical averages and human experiences to run in opposite directions. A *per capita* increase in quantitative factors may take place at the same time as a great qualitative disturbance in people's way of life. People may consume more goods, and become less happy or less free at the same time . . .

Over the period 1790–1840 there was a slight improvement in average material standards. Over the same period there was intensified exploitation, greater insecurity, and increasing human misery. By 1840 most people were 'better off' than their forerunners had been fifty years before, but they had suffered this slight improvement as a catastrophic experience.

From E.P. Thompson: *The Making of the English Working Class* (1963)

## K A.J. Taylor Indicates Problems of Measurement

We are here dealing with immeasurables but, because population growth and industrialisation came rapidly and the reaction to the problems which they created was relatively slow, it is hard to see that in the short run the Industrial Revolution did other than increase the sum of human misery for large sections of the population. It is necessary, nonetheless, to examine critically such suggestions as that the effect of industrialisation was to 'depersonalize' rather than to 'liberate' the individual. The psychological effects of any radical change in society are complex and their impact necessarily varies over time from individual to individual. The first half of the nineteenth century was a time when an old society was in travail to bring forth a new.

From A.J. Taylor: *The Standard of Living in Britain in the Industrial Revolution* (1975)

## L The Debate Continues

It is, of course, not to be expected that the debate will ever be resolved, no matter how much evidence is ultimately brought to bear on the issue. In part this is because the 'basket of goods' approach, however important, cannot capture the essence of such sweeping changes as industrialisation entails. Yet despite the dramatic evidence on the difficulties of transition, we must still ask about the alternatives available to society, as well as note that the 'quality of life' changed in both directions during this period.

From R.M. Hartwell & S. Engerman, 'Models of Immiseration: the theoretical basis of Pessimism', in A.J. Taylor: *The Standard of Living in Britain in the Industrial Revolution* (1975).

# *Questions*

1 Examine the implications of the views expressed in Sources A and B in the light of the data in Table 9.1. **(7 marks)**

2 To what extent do the trends indicated in Tables 9.2–9.4 confirm the assertions made in Source C? **(6 marks)**

3 What trends towards economic and social change are discernible in Tables 9.5–9.9? **(6 marks)**

**4** Compare and contrast the economic thinking expressed in Sources D-F. **(9 marks)**

**5** Analyse Sources G-L and suggest reasons why historians differ so widely in their views of the impact which industrialisation made upon the working-class standard of living. **(12 marks)**

# 10 CHARTISM – THE HISTORICAL DEBATE

Historians have posed five major questions relating to Chartism:
1. Was it an economic and social movement or a political one?
2. Was it a national movement?
3. Was the Chartist movement well led?
4. Was it a revolutionary movement?
5. Was it a success or a failure?

A review of the debate follows, dealing with each question in turn.

## 1 Was it an economic and social movement or a political one?

J.R. Stephens asserted that Chartism was a response to economic deprivation, a socio-economic view which was also held by Gammage. Later historians accepted this assumption with little question; G.D.H. Cole continued to do so in the 1940s. However, Cole guided the study of Chartism in two different directions: the Chartists themselves and the localities where Chartism flourished, rather than their ideas. A number of historians took up this challenge in the 1950s and significant local divergence among the Chartists began to emerge. In the 1960s E.P. Thompson stressed that the masses were capable of creating Chartism from their own intellectual resources, and this hastened a reassessment of the origins and nature of Chartism. Historians intensified their analysis of sources which related more to local Chartists rather than national Chartism, and Dorothy Thompson's thesis, that it was political rather than socio-economic in origin, seems to be well-established [A-G].

**A J.R. Stephens at Kersal Moor, Near Manchester (September 1838)**
This question of Universal Suffrage was a knife and fork question after all; this question was a bread and cheese question, and if any man asked him what he meant by Universal Suffrage, he would answer that every working man in the land had the right to have a good coat to his back, a comfortable abode in which to shelter himself and his family, a good dinner upon his table, and no more work than was necessary for keeping him in health, and as much wages for that work as would keep him in plenty, and afford him the blessings of life which a reasonable man could desire.

From *Northern Star*, 29 September 1838

## B Gammage Supports Stephens' Argument
It may be doubted whether there ever was a great political movement of the people without a social origin. The chief material object of mankind is to possess the means of social enjoyment. Secure them in the possession of these and small is the care they have for political abstractions. It is the existence of great social wrongs which principally teaches the masses the value of political rights.

From R.G. Gammage: *History of the Chartist Movement 1837–1854* (1854)

## C G.D.H. Cole – 'Hunger and Hatred'
Hunger and hatred – these were the forces that made Chartism a mass movement of the British working class. The new machines set a pace of output which reduced to dire penury those who were forced to compete with them. They flung men out of work by the thousands, and sent them to struggle wildly for jobs, at any wage the employer would offer and under any conditions of over-work. Hours of labour in the factories were stretched out to almost unbelievable lengths, throwing more workers out of jobs, and making the scramble worse.

From G.D.H. Cole: *Chartist Portraits* (1941)

## D Asa Briggs and Local Studies
Chartism was a snowball movement which gathered together local grievances and sought to give them common expression in a nation-wide agitation. Many of the internal conflicts which divided it had their origins in the differences of background and outlook in what the Chartists called 'the localities'. The differences ante-dated both the publication of the Charter and the onset of the business depression which gave the new movement its greatest momentum. Some of them had deep roots in pre-industrial history: others were associated with the growth of the machine industry.

From Asa Briggs: *Chartist Studies* (1959)

## E E.P. Thompson and Nineteenth-Century Working-Class Culture
We may describe popular Radicalism in these years [1780–1832] as an intellectual culture. The articulate consciousness of the self-taught was above all a political consciousness. For the first half of the nineteenth century, when the formal education of a great part of the people entailed little more than instruction in the Three R's, was by no means a period of intellectual atrophy. Given the elementary techniques of literacy, labourers, artisans, shopkeepers and clerks and schoolmasters, proceeded to instruct themselves, severally or in groups. And the books or instructors were very often those sanctioned by reforming opinion . . .

Recent studies have thrown much light on the predicament of the working-class reader in these years. We may say that something like two out of every three working men were able to read after some fashion in the early part of the century, although rather fewer could write. But the ability to read was only the elementary technique. The ability to handle abstract and consecutive argument was by no means inborn; it had to be discovered against almost overwhelming difficulties.

From E.P. Thompson: *The Making of the English Working Class* (1963)

### F Dorothy Thompson Argues that Chartism Was an Intellectual Response

It is an important part of Chartism to see it as the response of a literate and sophisticated working class. The response of a labour force faced with the arguments of the philosophical radicals and the political economists. Much of the Chartist propaganda took the form of argument, a dialogue with the middle classes. Although clearly not all Chartists could read and the level of literacy amongst those who could nominally read and write must often have been low, nevertheless written and printed material was an essential part of the lives of them all. Newspapers and pamphlets were available in even very small communities, at beer-houses, inns, coffee-shops, newsagents and each other's houses, journals were read and discussed.

From Dorothy Thompson: *The Early Chartists* (1971)

### G Rather than a Socio-economic One

Chartism came about because the people in different manufacturing districts found themselves agreed on the need for a movement to protect their existing institutions and achievements, to resist the attacks being mounted on them by the newly-enfranchised employing class, and to press forward for more freedoms and a more equitable form of taxation, employment and citizenship . . .

Chartism differed from earlier radical movements in scale more than in its programme. Its significance lay in its ability to hold together over a period of years a variety of impulses within a single programme, and to cover the whole of the British Isles in its appeal and its organisation.

From Dorothy Thompson: *The Chartists* (1984).

# 2 Was Chartism a national movement?

A number of features gave Chartism the appearance of a national movement. Early historians, such as Mark Hovell, assumed that it was so and by treating it as such drew general conclusions which distorted Chartist history for some years. In the 1950s when *Chartist Studies* was published it became clear that wide regional and local variations had existed within the movement. Since the 1970s attempts have been made to reconcile this local diversity with the view that Chartism was a national movement, and what seems to have emerged is that both dimensions, the local and the national, must be borne in mind for a full understanding of the movement [H-P].

## H Mark Hovell with a National Perspective

The Chartist Movement was a movement whose immediate object was political reform and whose ultimate purpose was social regeneration. Its programme of political reform was laid down in the 'People's Charter'. Its social aims were never defined, but they were sufficiently, though variously, described by leading men of the movement. It was a purely working-class movement, originating exclusively and drawing its whole following from the industrialised and unpropertied working class which had recently come into existence. For the most part it was a revolt of this body against intolerable conditions of existence. That is why its programme of social amelioration was vague and negative. It was an attempt on the part of the less educated portion of the community to legislate for a new and astounding condition of society whose evils the more enlightened portion had been either helpless or unwilling to remedy.

From Mark Hovell: *The Chartist Movement* (1918)

## I Local Variations

A study of Chartism must begin with a proper appreciation of regional and local diversity. Some of the elements of diversity are measurable – rents, wages, prices, the incidence of unemployment, the degree of dependence on foreign markets. Some however, cannot be measured quantitatively. Variations in local class structure, in the content of local grievances, in the traditions of political leadership and mass agitation, and in the adaptability and persistence of the Chartists and of their opponents require detailed investigation.

From Asa Briggs: *Chartist Studies* (1959)

**J Manchester**
Society in early industrial Manchester was centred almost exclusively
on its cotton industry. It lacked all the usual gentle gradations of
status and of wealth: masters and men faced each other almost alone.
At all times such social cleavage tended to social tension. But in the
late 1830s this tension was much increased by the general prevalence
of economic distress. This was the background of Manchester
Chartism. Operatives went hungry, while their employers patently did
not. Class conflict between cotton masters and cotton operatives
became the basis of the Chartist movement in Lancashire.

From Donald Read: 'Chartism in Manchester'. In *Chartist Studies*

**K Leeds**
Leeds Chartism was determined largely by its origins in earlier Radical
and working-class movements. But underlying these were distinctive
economic and social factors which also helped to give a somewhat
different basis to Chartism in Leeds, from that found elsewhere in
the West Riding. It did not have any large numbers of depressed
handworkers, and in this it was markedly different from other West
Riding towns such as Halifax and Bradford . . .
    Leeds Chartism became a movement of Radical small tradesmen
and artisans with its influence centred in the newer working-class
areas of the town. It was not a proletarian movement based on
handworkers, as at Bradford, nor a base for power of new national
leaders like Ernest Jones at Halifax. The existence of Chartist
councillors gave to the Leeds organisation a certain stability and
weight.

From J.F.C. Harrison: 'Chartism in Leeds'. In *Chartist Studies*

**L Leicester**
The close connection between Chartism and framework knitting is
shown clearly in two respects. First, there is a high degree of
correlation between the main centres of the industry and the places
from which there were reports of Chartist activity. Second, many of
the local Chartist leaders were framework knitters . . .
    Among the leaders of this type there [were] three marked
characteristics. They were all self-educated working men and small
tradesmen; a majority of them had a strong Nonconformist allegiance.
And many of them had had experience in Radical and working-class
movements of various kinds before 1838.

From J.F.C. Harrison: 'Chartism in Leicester'. In *Chartist Studies*

## M London

During the 1840s metropolitan Chartist culture appears to have been much the same as that of the major centres of Chartist activity in other parts of the country: with one outstanding exception. The Londoners tended to be non-religious or actively anti-Christian. Metropolitan rationalism was a deep-rooted characteristic both preceding and postdating Chartism. Chartism inherited another metropolitan tradition dating from the 1790s, that of insurrectionary conspiracy, with disastrous consequences in 1848 . . .

From David Goodway: *London Chartism 1838–1848* (1982)

## N Birmingham

The Birmingham district, though it included some big factories, was still mainly a region of small working masters, half independent and half subject to merchants who contracted to take their wares. Between these small masters and the skilled artisans who worked with them there was no sharp division of class. They could be combined, as they had been in the Reform struggle, under a common leadership; and this leadership was most likely to come from the Radical middle class.

From G.D.H. Cole: *Chartist Portraits* (1941)

## O Local and National Tensions

The pull between local and national activity was a central feature of Chartist politics. Although some associations followed the directives of the NCA executive with remarkable equanimity, others complained of neglect or interference.

From David Jones: *Chartism and the Chartists* (1975)

## P Chartism – a Local and a National Movement

With the publication of *Chartist Studies* (1959), there has been a serious attempt to get back to the local roots of Chartist protest. Asa Briggs noted that a proliferation of local Chartist histories was a prerequisite to any new narrative history of Chartism. Since then there has been such a proliferation. At its best, such local work has provided valuable insight into the character of rank-and-file Chartist activity; however, all too often, such studies have suffered from the lack of a national framework to which to relate local protest. Without losing sight of the locality as the centre of activity for most Chartists, an understanding of Chartism must take into account the attempt to transcend local diversity, to create a sense of national class consciousness and to establish a national political party of the working class.

From James Epstein: *The Lion of Freedom* (1982)

# 3 Was the Chartist movement well led?

The Chartist leaders themselves argued heatedly over this and therefore to a degree created the problem. Their admiration for each other was often tempered by bitter rivalry [4.A-L]. R.G. Gammage certainly allowed his personal feelings to affect his judgement. Chartist leaders naturally gave partisan views of the leadership quarrels. Unfortunately this suited the preconceptions which early writers held about the leaders; they preferred Lovett to O'Connor, because the former was balanced, moderate and respectable, and appeared to have his position of leader usurped by the unscrupulous, egocentric rabble-rouser. This led to a distorted interpretation of O'Connor's leadership. The universal distaste with which Feargus was depicted began to undergo modification in the early 1960s and the reassessment of him is continuing. Recent opinion has described him as the personification of Chartism, without whom the national aspects of the movement would have been unsustainable for as long as they were [Q-V]

## Q R.G. Gammage Discusses the Chartist Leaders
### Bronterre O'Brien
Of all the democratic leaders of the Chartist movement, he was undoubtedly the man with the greatest breadth of vision. His veriest foes bore testimony to the greatness of his intellect. The *Weekly Chronicle* described him as a man having more in his little finger than all the other Chartist leaders put together.
### William Lovett
He was the life and soul of that body [the LWMA]. Possessed of a clear and masterly intellect and great powers of application, everything he attempted was certain of accomplishment; and, though not by any means an orator, he was in matters of business more useful to the movement than those who were gifted with finer powers of speech.
### Ernest Jones
Jones maintained an attitude of dignified respect towards O'Connor; but it was only the prudence of the hypocrite which dictated his conduct. While Jones had not the courage to speak or write openly his real sentiments, he went about plotting in the dark to secure his [O'Connor's] overthrow.
### Feargus O'Connor
If ever men deserved to be classed among cowards and poltroons, and to meet with the scorn and derision of mankind, it must be frankly confessed by all readers of Irish history that the kings of Ireland were entitled to that distinction, and none more so than the ancestors of O'Connor.

He showed himself to be either cowardly or treacherous towards those whom he styled his friends. A love of popularity was the besetting sin of the latter [O'Connor]. To win and retain that popularity, with O'Connor all means were justifiable.

From R.G. Gammage: *History of the Chartist Movement 1837–1854* (1854)

### R Hovell Finds O'Connor Unlikeable

The immense exertions of O'Connor in the cause of the poor, vain, futile, and self-glorifying as those exertions were, were nevertheless a passport to the affection of many thousands of followers.

There is a repulsive aspect in the manner in which O'Connor exploited this. That [it] did not exhaust the affection is a witness to the intensity of feeling and the blind ignorance of the followers . . .

It would be idle to suppose that O'Connor in no way deserved this fidelity; men do not gain such homage without cause or merit. But O'Connor's character was such that no man of independence, talents, and integrity could long cooperate with him.

From Mark Hovell: *The Chartist Movement* (1918)

### S An Objective Assessment

O'Connor's egocentricity can be conceded at once. He wanted to be the unquestioned leader. Yet as soon as the Charter was launched a demagogue leader was needed. Lovett could not play the part: O'Connor was excellently equipped to do so . . .

In creating the Chartist movement as a popular agitation, O'Connor contributed little original philosophy, although he often liked to pose as a theorist. But [he] was not the first, nor the last, politician to advocate foolish policies.

Another charge against O'Connor has been that his language was exaggerated. Three lines of defence are open here. Firstly all popular movements require loud language to keep them going. Secondly, we must not forget the terrible conditions of the time. Finally, up to a point at least, it was deliberate bluff. O'Connor knew, as Lovett did not, that government would never concede the Charter to a quiet movement. He hoped to frighten them.

From Read & Glasgow: *Feargus O'Connor. Irishman and Chartist* (1961)

### T O'Connor's Leadership Qualities

As Chartism's most prominent national leader, O'Connor played a central role in maintaining the movement's national challenge. He was able to unite the forces of Chartism behind his leadership. [His] popularity was based on his unrivalled talents as an agitator, his brilliance as an orator, his indefatigable energy in the radical cause; but his standing within the ranks of Chartism was also founded upon the consistent and intelligent leadership which he had provided since the mid-1830s. He came to symbolise the independence of working-class political struggle.

From James Epstein: *The Lion of Freedom* (1982)

## U The Importance of His Leadership
Of the importance of Feargus O'Connor as a national leader, there can be no question . . .

O'Connor has been seen as the evil genius of the movement. In fact, so far from being the exploiter and distorter of the movement, O'Connor was so much the centre of it that, had the name Chartism not been coined, the radical movement between 1838 and 1848 must surely have been called O'Connorite Radicalism. Remove him and his newspaper and the movement fragments, localises and loses its continuity.

From Dorothy Thompson: *The Chartists* (1984)

## V His Superiority over His Rivals
No one matched O'Connor in the qualities demanded of a national leader. He was a superb platform speaker with a splendid presence, wonderfully racy and vivid in his language, and wildly funny both on the platform and in his writings. Many historians have seen only his braggadocio, the bombastic expression of prophecies and claims that could never be fulfilled. But much more important was the confidence that [he] generated among the poor and down-trodden. It was this crucial belief in the righteousness of the cause, and his ability to communicate it in unqualified terms, that allowed O'Connor to tower above his fellow Chartists.

From John Saville: *1848* (1987)

# 4 Was Chartism a revolutionary movement?

The contemporary fear of Chartism suggests to us that it sought a violent revolution [8.C-J]. Leading speakers of the day seem to confirm this with the extreme language which they used, but historians experience some difficulty with this question. The 'moral' force and 'physical' force split indicates that the movement had its violent side, but historians tend to differ on its importance. The current consensus is that the Chartists sought a bloodless revolution, though a revolution nonetheless [W-Bb].

## W Dorothy Thompson Considers the National Conspiracy

After the ending of the Convention [in 1839] an underground movement developed, meeting secretly, gathering arms, and planning either an insurrection or armed resistance to an anticipated government attack. Such work as has been done on this 'underground' has of course met with difficulties greater than even those involved in recording the public or semi-public activities of the Chartists. Much remains to be discovered. Much may never now be discovered. Of the existence of a national conspiracy there can be little doubt, although its extent and the involvement of national leaders remain to be teased out from a mass of contradictory evidence. The one event which has entered all the records was the Newport rising of November 1839.

From Dorothy Thompson: *The Chartists* (1984)

## X Hovell Had Seen It Differently

It was not a revolutionary movement, nor were its leaders. It is true that there were real revolutionaries among them, but their time had not yet come. The true revolutionary does not give way to rhetoric. Mere words will not satisfy him, and we have no evidence that either Stephens, Oastler or O'Connor was prepared to go beyond mere words. Their business was protest.

From Mark Hovell: *The Chartist Movement* (1918)

## Y The Menace of Armed Chartism

Beyond the Convention, many Chartists had for months advocated recourse to physical violence. Up and down the country reports spread of militant groups hoarding pikes, spears and muskets for the coming revolution. After making all allowance for the exaggerations, it is certain that considerable numbers of men had taken anti-Poor Law and Chartist militants at their word. And declining industrial conditions enhanced urban militancy in some areas. As a result, in many places Chartism took on the menacing aspect of a terrorist organisation.

From J.T. Ward: *Chartism* (1973)

## Z The Limits of Insurgency

Certainly, the extent of open insurrection was remarkably small. Chartists took up arms only in exceptional circumstances. One obvious source of political militancy were communities with a long tradition of violent action. When Chartism reached these 'hell-holes', and invaded the out-townships of large cities, violent language and the shooting of firearms were an immediate and natural accompaniment. Here sufficient sanctions and underground organisations existed to make a concerted rising possible. The great fear was that Chartists would become acknowledged spokesmen for these violent communities.

From David Jones: *Chartism and the Chartists* (1975)

### Aa The Chartist Belief in a Bloodless Revolution
All assumed that the necessary changes in class legislation would follow working-class representation at Westminster. The institutions of the state, so it was believed, could and would respond to the people's representatives. At the same time, the Chartist movement took it for granted, that the achievement of the Six Points would be the first major step towards a new kind of social order.

From John Saville: *1848* (1987)

### Bb Part of the Chartist procession to Kennington Common, April 1848

PART OF THE PROCESSION.—SKETCHED AT BLACKFRIARS-BRIDGE.

# 5 Was Chartism a success or a failure?

It was certainly in the interests of the authorities to depict it as a failure, and public condemnation and ridicule was used to great effect to suggest it was so in 1848. The later nineteenth-century view accepted that verdict although early twentieth-century commentators suggested different criteria for assessment. They argued that whether the Chartists won their Six Points or not, was of less importance than the creation of a mass movement through which working men and women perceived that their conditions could be improved. More recently, the Chartists' formation of the movement has been acclaimed as their outstanding and singular achievement [Cc-Ff].

### Cc The Official Verdict after 1848
Chartism was finally broken by the physical force of the state, and having once been broken it was submerged, in the national consciousness, beneath layers of false understanding and denigration. What was quite forgotten was the strength that continued in Chartism and even the mass arrests and jailings were wiped from public memory. The contemporary media were extraordinarily effective in traducing this greatest of all mass movements of the nineteenth century.

From John Saville: *1848* (1987)

### Dd Hovell Questions that Verdict
Contemporaries had no hesitation in declaring the movement fruitless. The judgement of its own age has been accepted by many later historians, and there has been general agreement in placing Chartism among the lost causes of history . . .
In the long run Chartism by no means failed. On its immediate political side the principles of the Charter have gradually become parts of the British constitution. If on its broader social aspects there was no such vindication, this is due partly to the fact that the Chartists had no social policy in the sense that they had a political platform.

From Mark Hovell: *The Chartist Movement* (1918)

### Ee A Contemporary of Hovell Uses Different Criteria
The Chartist movement was the first organised effort to stir up class consciousness on a national scale. Judged by its crop of statutes and statues, Chartism was a failure. Judged by its essential and generally overlooked purpose, Chartism was a success. It achieved not the Six Points, but a state of mind.

From Julius West: *A History of the Chartist Movement* (1920)

### Ff The Chartists' Achievement – Chartism

Indeed Chartism did make a powerful political impact, bringing a new urgency to the philanthropic impulses of private individuals and the reforming tendencies of those in government – though to a list of social reforms should be added the introduction and implementation of legislation extending police forces to many parts of the provinces, a Chartist achievement but never a Chartist aim! The quest for Chartist achievement has also led sometimes to a listing of enactments of the later nineteenth and twentieth centuries, by which many points of the Charter were granted, but this seems fallacious. Those Acts cannot even remotely be attributed to Chartist pressure, and the real spirit of democracy which lay behind the points of the Charter remains unrealised even in the later twentieth century. The positive achievements of the Chartists are to be found not in legislation, passed at the time or in the remoter future, but in the mobilisation of the considerable mental, spiritual and emotional capacities of the working men and women of early Industrial Britain. The Chartists' greatest achievement was Chartism, a movement shot through not with despair but with hope.

From Edward Royle: *Chartism* (1980)

# Questions

1 Examine Sources A-G and explain why the view expressed in Source E might be regarded as a turning point in the study of the origins of the Chartist movement. **(12 marks)**

2 In what respects do Sources I-P challenge the assumption of Source H? **(12 marks)**

3 Study Sources Q-V and explain why the assessment of O'Connor in Sources Q-R has been modified in Sources S-V. **(12 marks)**

4 'For historians of the Chartist movement the term "revolution" is a major pitfall.' Examine this statement in reference to Sources W-Aa. **(12 marks)**

5 What are the different criteria used in Sources Cc-Ff in assessing the success or failure of the Chartists? **(12 marks)**

# 11 DEALING WITH EXAMINATION QUESTIONS

## Specimen Answers to Source-based Questions

*Questions based on Chapter 7 – 'Chartists and the Land' (See pages 70–79).*

## Questions

**1** Using Source F, and your own knowledge, explain why the Chartist Land Plan was implemented. **(4 marks)**

**2** In what ways do Sources J and S differ in their views as to how the land might be used to improve the condition of the working class? **(7 marks)**

**3** With reference to Source V, indicate some of the social problems which prevailed during the Chartist period. **(7 marks)**

**4** Consider the value to the historian of Sources J, V, and S as evidence of disunity among the Chartists. **(8 marks)**

**5** Describe the later history of the Land Plan and consider its contribution to the Chartist movement. **(9 marks)**

### Points to note about these questions

**1** A direct question carrying relatively few marks. It demands a concise response, drawn from both the source and the candidate's background knowledge.

**2** A response based upon the two sources is required here. Although this seems to be an easier question than 1, it demands a close study of the sources to pick out the implications within them.

**3** This is a straightforward question, the answer to which is contained in the source. Close study of the source is required to ensure the candidate includes all the points which Jones makes.

**4** As is suggested by the number of marks allocated, this is a more complex question. In addition to the different views on land as expressed in the sources, there were other divisive issues not mentioned in the extracts to which reference must be made.

**5** This type of question makes great demands upon the candidate's knowledge of the subject. Here the examinee must place the sources in an historical context.

# Specimen Answers

**1** Using Source F, and your own knowledge, explain why the Chartist Land Plan was implemented. **(4 marks)**

Source F suggests that the Land Plan aimed at freeing workers from the wage system by making them economically independent of employers and furthering the cause of Chartism generally. The failure of the second petition in 1842 and the government's repression of the movement after the 'Plug Plot' strikes, had left the movement in a weakened condition. The Land Plan, first suggested by O'Connor in 1843, was an attempt to give the movement a new focus.

**2** In what ways do Sources J and S differ in their views as to how the land might be used to improve the condition of the working class? **(7 marks)**

O'Brien's view of the land is a more comprehensive one than that of O'Connor. The former saw the land as one of several sectors of the economy, which would become state-controlled in the interests of all the people, when a new social system emerged out of the granting of the Charter. The latter regarded the land as a way of securing the Charter, and based his view on the enrichment of the quality of the individual working man's life within the existing system.

**3** With reference to Source V, indicate some of the social problems which prevailed during the Chartist period. **(7 marks)**

Source V refers to mass poverty generally and to its symptoms and causes in particular. It condemns the idea of small landed proprietors, because this would do nothing to break the control of the large landlords over agriculture. It considers the allocation of unused land among the destitute as a major improvement on the existing system of poor relief, set up in the Poor Law of 1834. It would eradicate the need for the building of 'Bastilles' to provide indoor relief for paupers, and would relieve the labour market of large numbers of unemployed who formed a pool of cheap labour, which forced down wage levels. It would also stop the flow of emigrants from the United Kingdom, which by 1852 was becoming a serious problem, exacerbated by the Irish potato famine of the late 1840s.

**4** Consider the value to the historian of Sources J, V, and S as evidence of disunity among the Chartists. **(8 marks)**

Source J gives a socialist view of land utilisation. Source V perceives land-use as only a partial solution of the endemic poverty which beset the working class in the first half of the nineteenth century. In contrast, Source S emphasises the independence of spirit which the ownership of land would give families suffering under the rigid discipline of the wage system and the factories. Each source presents a contrary view, and the historian would be able to discern the divisive nature of the land question from them. O'Brien and O'Connor argued bitterly over the question when the Land Plan was first proposed, while Jones, after initially supporting O'Connor's plan, began to move away from it. However, Jones, a latecomer to Chartism, and O'Brien, who had been a Chartist from the beginning, argued bitterly at a personal level. O'Brien's quarrel with O'Connor had personal elements in it. O'Brien became more resentful of his compatriot after they were both released from prison in the early 1840s. The movement split at this time over the question of the 'New Move'; a series of proposals to reappraise the Chartist strategy after the setbacks of 1839. One of the major 'New Movers' was William Lovett, a moderate Chartist who felt that the workers must raise their standards of education and social behaviour in order to earn the Charter. He was opposed by O'Connor and others who demanded the Charter as a right, irrespective of social acceptability. This dispute took place even before 1839, and therefore the movement lacked unity from its very birth. Sources J, V and S do little to indicate the extent of disunity, nor the severe personal dislikes at leadership level. Consequently, the historian studying disunity within the movement generally would need additional sources dealing with issues other than the land question.

**5** Describe the later history of the Land Plan and consider its contribution to the Chartist movement. **(9 marks)**

The Land Plan had some success in setting up five 'O'Connorvilles' after May 1847. They folded after 1851, when the Land Company was wound up by Act of Parliament. The legality of the Company had always been in question and many of its opponents, such as Thomas Cooper the Leicester leader, had warned O'Connor of the risks he was running. After the 'fiasco' of 1848 a parliamentary select committee inquired into the management of the company which was declared illegal and dissolved in August 1851. The estates which were established failed for many reasons – not least, the over-optimistic forecasts regarding both the increase in land values and in the amount of produce which the land would yield. The consequence was that the anticipated resources, earmarked for funding further 'O'Connorvilles', did not materialise.

The failure of the settlements was regarded by contemporaries as proof that the plan was ill-considered and impractical. However, it played a significant role within the movement and should be seen not as a hare-brained scheme but as one of a number of self-help initiatives, including the co-operative movement, which were adopted by groups of workers during the 1840s. In its short life the Chartist Land Association amassed some 70,000 members in 240 branches throughout the country. The 'O'Connorvilles' helped to stimulate and sustain this growth through their initial success, and the Association kept Chartism alive during the fallow period from 1843 to 1848 when the movement seemed to be in decline.

It is true that the plan was divisive and impractical, but like the Charter itself it had a unifying function and became a focal point for Chartists whose spirits were flagging after 1842. It renewed hope that the present condition of England was not a permanent one, and, perhaps more importantly, it nourished hope among industrial workers, who were, at most, but one generation removed from rural life.

### Key points to note in the answers

**1** Two points are made; the first arises directly from the source, the second relates to Chartism generally.

**2** There is no straying from the documents here; understanding of the two sources is demonstrated by highlighting how they differ from each other.

**3** Although attention is directed towards the document, it is interpreted against a broader knowledge of the period; e.g. the Poor Law Amendment Act of 1834 and the landlord system of land holding.

**4** The limitation of the sources is emphasised by pointing out that they relate to only one of the divisive issues among Chartists. This shows that, in addition to knowledge, the candidate has an understanding that the question relates to Chartist disunity generally.

**5** Relevance to the subject of the sources is important here, but it would not have been sufficient merely to note and explain the collapse of the Land Plan. The answer places the Plan in the context not only of Chartism but also of working-class initiatives during the period.

# Preparing Essay Answers

The reports of the examination boards point out every year that the greatest single weakness among examinees is an inability to respond relevantly. No matter how well read and knowledgeable candidates may be, if they stray too far from the terms of the question they cannot be given credit. Examinations from A Level upwards are basically a test of the candidates' ability to analyse historical material in such a manner as to present a reasoned, informed, response to a specific question. Too often examiners are faced with regurgitated notes on a set of topics, little of which relates to the questions as set. There really is no such animal as an 'easy' exam question at these levels; those who set the papers seldom repeat the exact wording of their questions. This means that each question demands its own individual interpretation. The intelligence and subtlety of the candidates' response will determine how high a mark they score. Examinees must, of course, have 'knowledge', but academic history tests not only what they know but how well they use what they know.

As an aid to the development of effective examination technique, here is a list of questions that candidates should ask themselves when preparing their essays:

**1** *Have I answered the questions AS SET* or have I simply imposed my prepared answer on it? (It is remarkable how many exam scripts contain answers to questions that do not appear on the exam paper!)

**2** *Have I produced a genuine argument* or have I merely put down a number of disconnected points in the hope that the examiners can work it out for themselves? (Too many answers consist of a list of facts rounded off by the 'Thus it can be seen . . .' type of statement which seldom relates to what has been previously written.)

**3** *Have I been relevant in arguing my case* or have I included ideas and facts that have no real relation to the question? (Some candidates simply write down all they know about a topic, assuming that sheer volume will overwhelm the examiner into giving a satisfactory mark. This 'mud-at-the-wall' method is counter-productive since it glaringly exposes the candidate's inability to be selective or show judgement.

**4** *Have I made appropriate use of primary or secondary sources to illustrate my answer?* (Examiners do look for evidence of intelligent reading. Choice, apt, quotation from documents or books does elevate the quality of an answer. Acquaintance with the ideas of modern historians and authorities is a hallmark of the better prepared candidate. However, discretion needs to be shown; putting in quotations where they are not relevant or inserting over-long, rote-learned passages merely looks like padding.)

**5** *Have I tried to show originality* or have I just played safe and written a dull, uninspired answer? (Remember, examiners have to plough through vast quantities of dreary, ill-digested material from large numbers of candidates. When, therefore, they come across a script that shows initiative and zest, their interest and sympathy are engaged. A candidate who applies his own reasoning and interpretation to a question may occasionally make naive statements but, given that his basic understanding and knowledge are sound, his ambition will be rewarded. This is not an encouragement to 'waffle' but it is to suggest that, provided always that he keeps to the terms of the question, the candidate is free to follow his own judgements. A thought-provoking answer is likely to be a good answer.)

# *Possible Essay Titles*

**1** Analyse the origins of the Chartist movement.

It would be inadequate merely to consider the economic changes of the period. The origins of the six points must be included, so too the radical causes of the 1830s. Working-class awareness and understanding of the ideas underlying the Charter need discussion. Some evaluation of the relative importance of all these factors must be made to score highly.

**2** 'The People's Charter was not an end in itself, more a means to achieving a number of different ends.' Discuss.

This question relates to the six points, and the role they played in uniting the movement. It is important to stress the variety of goals which Chartists sought beyond the Charter. The strength of each goal should be assessed.

**3** How far may Chartism be regarded as a revolutionary movement?

This question goes far beyond the Moral v. Physical Force debate. Candidates must consider the term 'revolutionary'. It might be treated in several ways; firstly in the conventional sense of a violent revolution like that of 1789 in France; secondly it might be treated as a constitutional revolution merely demanding changes which would 'revolutionise' the political system; thirdly, in the Marxist view of 'revolution'; seeing it as the first organised proletarian movement, demonstrating a growing class consciousness encouraged by the repressive reaction of a bourgeois government.

**4** Was Chartism a national movement?

Chartism's national characteristics can be established by reference to the Charter as a focal point for protest and discontent; the nationwide organisation required for simultaneous meetings, the NCA, and the Conventions. The local nature of the movement can be demonstrated by looking at various centres and pointing out the variety in ideology and social mix of the membership. Differences within localities like London will strengthen the point. Some conclusion as to the relative strength of local and national loyalties is needed.

**5** 'Feargus O'Connor was Chartism.' Is this an accurate description of the movement's leadership?

The recent re-appraisal of O'Connor's function is relevant here. The traditional view that he was egocentric and intolerant of opposition from other leaders needs to be sketched. The adulation which the members bestowed upon him would need to be set against that. His role of maintaining Chartist unity and momentum are essential. Whether the quotation is an overstatement or not is for the candidate to decide.

**6** What problems does the identification of the rank and file supporters of Chartism present to the historian?

The candidate must avoid the cliche that Chartist rank and file were handloom weavers displaced by the development of the power-loom. Some Chartists doubtless were, but the question asks how the others might be identified. Anonymity was the common characteristic of ordinary Chartists, and this demands a quantitative approach and some mention of the sources available should be made. Links with other working-class organisations such as trade unions, co-operatives, and Owenite groups can be established. The strength of the membership within the manufacturing communities compared with the large urban centres is equally important.

**7** Examine the contention that, 'by 1848 the mass demonstration was an outmoded form of political activity'.

This is not simply about the Kennington Common meeting of 1848. It is concerned with the growing state apparatus for maintaining order which had been developing for half a century. Reference to pre-Chartist disturbances would be admissible to strengthen the point, as would the growing use of police and the military to control huge meetings. Mention should be made of Chartist leaders' awareness that leading unarmed crowds against heavily armed security forces was futile. Mass events aimed to intimidate the authorities, by 1848 it was the crowds who had become intimidated.

**8** Was Chartism a class movement?

The origins of the movement are relevant to this question for they stem from working-class grievances, such as the poor law. The effects of the great betrayal of 1832 upon class relationships should be referred to; so too should middle-class involvement in the first petition and the alienation of such radicals by the violent tone of Chartist rhetoric and the Newport rising. By 1840 the movement was essentially working-class and the rejection of the New Move underlines this point. Reference should be made to Engels' opinion of Chartism, with perhaps some discussion of what he meant by class.

**9** In what respects may Chartism be regarded as a failure?

It would be inadequate to list the six points and indicate when five of them were attained. The function which Chartism fulfilled was far more complex. Its failures included the loss of independence in education, and the centralisation of power through government apparatus, both of which Chartists hoped to prevent. The manufacturing communities where Chartism was strongest were absorbed into the great conurbations. On the credit side it focused attention upon a variety of grievances and aspirations and during the Chartist years other working-class organisations developed, with more limited aims and strong elements of self-help.

**10** Was Chartism dead by 1848?

The 'fiasco' of 1848, largely a myth, was created by both government and press and led to the notion that Chartism was ridiculed to death with the rejection of the third petition. Discussion of this and why it was felt necessary to certify Chartism's death should be discussed. The later history of the movement in its much weakened condition, and led by Ernest Jones down to 1858, when it merged with the radical reform movement, needs full treatment. Some conclusion relating to those years would need to be drawn.

# Specimen Essay Answer

### What was the significance of the role played by women within the Chartist Movement?

Until recently the role of women Chartists has been neglected by historians. This may be explained in part by the anxiety of early chroniclers, such as Gammage, that the movement be taken seriously by commentators and that a reflection of the full part women played might open it to ridicule. The forceful and aggressive woman was regarded in the mid-nineteenth century as in some way unfeminine, not to say unnatural, and therefore women Chartists were largely ignored.

Historians such as Dorothy Thompson have endeavoured to correct this distortion and we now have a clearer view of women Chartists. Their role changed as the movement developed. In the early years, down to about 1843, they played a prominent part at processions and demonstrations, usually leading the array of banners and flags which they had fashioned. They rarely spoke from platforms on these occasions. Although some public speakers such as Mary Anne Walker, Susanna Inge and Mary Grasby highlighted the problems women faced, the solutions they advocated were applicable generally to the working class irrespective of gender. Women attended indoor meetings, even those held in local alehouses, for it had long been the practice of working-class women to smoke and drink as part of their leisure activities. Some time during the 1840s this powerful public presence declined, possibly for two reasons: firstly, the meetings became increasingly violent, as Chartists clashed with the authorities and the apparatus for maintaining public order became more effective; secondly, the socially acceptable stereotype of female behaviour in which women became more passive, 'modest' and less 'bold' began to permeate a working class which increasingly adopted the 'respectable' image of propertied-class women.

In the period down to the 'Plug' strikes of 1842 over 100 women's organisations were set up to press for the People's Charter, typically that of Newcastle and East London. It is significant that they were not advocates of changing the female role within the patriarchal family; in London the discussion of the marriage laws was discouraged by women at women's meetings. Their self-image was one of help-mate to their menfolk, and their resentment of the social changes which industrialisation wrought stemmed from the difficulties they faced in fulfilling their wife-mother role adequately, because they were being forced out of the home to work long and exhausting hours in factories and mines. Their grievances were those factors which damaged family life; the poverty which prevented them from providing a comfortable family home; the press-gang, which might shatter a family by the forcible removal of the man of the house to the armed forces; above all, the new Poor Law which forced the destitute into workhouses where families were split up.

The original draft of the Charter contained a demand for female suffrage. This was omitted, ostensibly lest it diverted attention from the main goal of the six points. However, Chartism was clearly a male-dominated movement and not all male members would have the liberal attitude of Lovett and Collins who advocated sexual equality. There is something patronising about even the most fervent supporters of female suffrage; R.J. Richardson seemed to decry the labour women were forced to perform in the new industrial society partly because it defeminised them. To a large extent, therefore, the public role of Chartist women was effected by the early-Victorian perception of what the ideal woman should be and how she should conduct herself. Women themselves were more concerned with the practical problems which they faced. They brought those problems into sharp focus by their organisation and presented several modes of action, perhaps the most significant being that of exclusive dealing which was a singularly female activity, as women tended to be the family shoppers.

Women played a vital part in Chartist education. They created schools where 'Chartism' could be taught as an alternative to the established educational orthodoxy, in which children were taught to accept things as they were, rather than how they might be improved. Wherever Chartist organisation was strong, the part played by women was proportionately potent; this indicates that their organisational function, even after their public role waned, was vital and without it Chartism could not have attained the status of a mass-movement.

# BIBLIOGRAPHY

**Clive Behagg:** *Labour and Reform: Working-Class Movements 1815–1914* (Hodder & Stoughton 1991).
This book has been written specifically for A-level and Higher Grade students, and combines useful narrative and analysis of working-class political agitation, along with exercises.

**ed. Asa Briggs:** *Chartist Studies* (Macmillan 1959).
A valuable collection of local studies illustrating Chartism's diversity.

**G.D.H. Cole:** *Chartist Portraits* (Macmillan 1965).
Somewhat dated, but containing useful biographical details of the leaders.

**James Epstein:** *The Lion of Freedom: Feargus O'Connor and the Chartist Movement, 1832–1842* (Croom Helm 1982).
An important reappraisal of O'Connor's leadership.

**eds. James Epstein and Dorothy Thompson:** *The Chartist Experience. Studies in Working-Class Radicalism and Culture 1830–1860* (Macmillan 1982).
A symposium of recent scholarship reassessing Chartism from a variety of viewpoints.

**David Goodway:** *London Chartism 1838–1848* (CUP 1982).
A major study of metropolitan Chartism, challenging many traditional assumptions.

**David Jones:** *Chartism and the Chartists* (Allen Lane 1975).
An indispensable examination of the Chartists and their problems.

**Alfred Plummer:** *Bronterre: A Political Biography of Bronterre O'Brien, 1806–1864* (University of Toronto Press 1971).
A full examination of the man, his life, and his ideas.

**Edward Royle:** *Chartism* (Longman 1980).
An analysis of the Chartism movement, combined with contemporary documentary material.

**John Saville:** *1848, The British State and the Chartist Movement* (CUP 1987).
A penetrating analysis of the development of the forces of public order against which Chartists were pitted.

**A.R. Schoyen:** *The Chartist Challenge, A Portrait of George Julian Harney* (Heinemann 1958).
Less than recent, this remains the definitive work on a much neglected though very significant Chartist leader, with youth on his side.

**Dorothy Thompson:** *The Chartists* (Temple Smith 1984).
A full and thorough study, containing many new approaches; particularly valuable are the sections on women in the movement and the nature of the rank and file membership.

**E.P. Thompson:** *The Making of the English Working Class* (Pelican 1968, 1st edn 1963).
The seminal work on the background to the movement.

**J.T. Ward:** *Chartism* (Batsford 1973).
A general study of the movement, dealing with its problems and its ideas.

# Acknowledgements

The Publishers would like to thank the following for permission to reproduce copyright illustrations in this volume:
'Work' by Ford Maddox Brown, 1865, Manchester City Art Galleries cover; Bishopsgate Institute p. 14; Leicestershire Museum, Art Galleries and Records Services p. 25, p. 84; Punch Publications p. 34, p. 44, p. 68; David Jones p. 56, p. 76; The Illustrated London News p. 109.

The Publishers would also like to thank the following for permission to reproduce material in this volume:
B T Batsford Ltd for the extract from J T Ward *Chartism* (Batsford. 1973); Cambridge University Press for the extract from John Saville *1848: The British State and the Chartist Movement* (CUP, 1987), and for the extracts from David Goodway *London Chartism 1838–1848* (CUP, 1982); Edward Arnold for the extract from Read and Glasgow *Feargus O'Connor: Irishman and Chartist* (Edward Arnold, 1961); Gower Publishing Group for the extract from Dorothy Thompson *The Chartists* (Temple Smith, 1984); Longman Group UK for the extract from Edward Royle *Chartism* (Longman, 1980); Methuen and Co. for the extract from A J Taylor *The Standard of Living in Britain in the Industrial Revolution* (Methuen, 1975); University of Toronto Press for the extract from Alfred Plummer *Bronterre: A Political Biography of Bronterre O'Brien 1806–1864* (University of Toronto Press, 1971); Victor Gollancz Ltd for the extracts from E P Thompson *The Making of the English Working Class* (Pelican, 1968).

Every effort has been made to trace and acknowledge ownership of copyright. The publishers will be glad to make suitable arrangements with any copyright holders whom it has not been possible to contact.

# INDEX

## Index